Teacher's Guide
Rapid Catch-up for Age 7+

William Collins' dream of knowledge for all began with the publication of his first book in 1819.
A self-educated mill worker, he not only enriched millions of lives, but also founded a flourishing publishing house.
Today, staying true to this spirit, Collins books are packed with inspiration, innovation and practical expertise.
They place you at the centre of a world of possibility and give you exactly what you need to explore it.

Collins. Freedom to teach.

Published by Collins

An imprint of HarperCollins*Publishers*
The News Building, 1 London Bridge Street, London, SE1 9GF, UK

HarperCollins*Publishers*
Macken House, 39/40 Mayor Street Upper, Dublin 1, D01 C9W8, Ireland

Browse the complete Collins catalogue at
collins.co.uk

© Wandle Learning Trust 2022
www.littlewandlelettersandsounds.org.uk

All trademarks in the Collins Big Cat logo © HarperCollins*Publishers* Limited

10 9 8 7 6 5 4 3 2

ISBN 978-0-00-856759-0

All rights reserved. No part of this publication may be reproduced, stored in a retrieval system, or transmitted in
any form by any means, electronic, mechanical, photocopying, recording or otherwise, without the prior written permission of
the Publisher or a licence permitting restricted copying in the United Kingdom issued by the
Copyright Licensing Agency Ltd, 5th Floor, Shackleton House, 4 Battle Bridge Lane, London SE1 2HX.

Without limiting the exclusive rights of any author, contributor or the publisher of this publication, any unauthorised use
of this publication to train generative artificial intelligence (AI) technologies is expresslyprohibited. HarperCollins also
exercise their rights under Article 4(3) of the Digital Single Market Directive 2019/790 and expressly reserve this
publication from the text and data mining exception.

British Library Cataloguing-in-Publication Data
A catalogue record for this publication is available from the British Library.

Authors: Charlotte Raby and Tracy Kewley
Publisher: Lizzie Catford
Copyeditor: Tracy Kewley
Proofreader: Faye Cheeseman
Cover designer: Steve Evans
Internal designer and typesetter: Pascal Don
Illustrator: Noah Warnes
Production controller: Katharine Willard
Printed and Bound in the UK by Ashford Colour Ltd

This book contains FSC™ certified paper and other controlled
sources to ensure responsible forest management.

For more information visit: www.harpercollins.co.uk/green

Wandle Learning Trust and Little Sutton Primary School have partnered with HarperCollins*Publishers* to provide teachers with
a full systematic synthetic phonics programme, Little Wandle Letters and Sounds Revised, and accompanying Collins Big Cat
readers. Full details of the programme, including CPD training, can be found at www.littlewandlelettersandsounds.org.uk.

Contents

Introducing Little Wandle Rapid Catch-up for age 7+	04
Identifying children for Rapid Catch-up	05
Using the assessment materials	05
Pathways	05
Assessment of progress	08
Exiting the programme	08
Organising and timetabling Rapid Catch-up	09
Rapid Catch-up progression	10
Teaching Rapid Catch-up	12
A word about the schwa	13
How to use the resources	14
Lesson templates	18
Phase 2	18
Phase 3	20
Phase 4	22
Phase 5	25
Prompt cards and 'How to' videos	28
Prompt cards: Quick review	30
Prompt cards: Teach and practise	32
Prompt cards: Practise and apply	49
Prompt card: Review lesson	53
Prompt cards: Reading practice sessions	54
Phase 2 grapheme chart	62
List of Phase 4 words	65
Phase 5 linked graphemes in order	66
Graphemes with more than one sound	69
Precision teaching grids	70

A downloadable version of this guide is available at collins.co.uk/RapidCatchUpTeacherGuide/download

Introducing Little Wandle Rapid Catch-up for age 7+

Every child in Year 2 or above who cannot read at age-related expectations needs urgent targeted support so that they can access the curriculum and enjoy reading as soon as possible.

Little Wandle Rapid Catch-up is a complete catch-up programme that mirrors the core phonics programme but has a faster pace. It has been created to help children catch up quickly. This quote from the Reading framework (2023) makes it clear why this is so important:

'After Year 1, learning in the wider curriculum depends increasingly on literacy. Pupils who cannot read well enough do not have full access to the curriculum. Those who fail to learn to read early on often start to dislike reading. They read less than others – and less often – and do not accumulate the background knowledge and vocabulary from reading that their peers do. The word-rich get richer, while the word-poor get poorer.'

In addition to this Teacher's guide, the Rapid Catch-up programme includes the following:

Printed books and resources from Collins:
- Decodable books matched exactly to the Rapid Catch-up programme, including blending practice books for Phases 2, 3 and 4
- Rapid Catch-up word cards and tricky word cards for all phases.

On the Little Wandle website at www.littlewandlelettersandsounds.org.uk:
- Rapid Catch-up assessment tools
- Rapid Catch-up weekly grids
- Rapid Catch-up 'How to' videos
- other teaching resources and guidance including images, weekly spellings and information for parents.

All of the resources have been designed to work seamlessly with existing Little Wandle resources such as the grapheme cards and picture cards, and the grapheme charts and mats.

Little Wandle Rapid Catch-up has been trialled in schools with high levels of EAL and Pupil Premium so that we can be sure that it provides the support needed to develop language alongside teaching reading words.

The programme has been developed to ensure plenty of repeated practice in blending, word reading and spelling in each lesson, using a range of activities such as **Change it**, **Match the words to the pictures** and **Mix it up**. Children also need to learn the meaning of the words that they read, which is why we provide simple definitions or contextualising sentences for words.

By the end of the programme children should be reading with enough fluency and accuracy to access the curriculum in class, and to read with enjoyment and understanding.

Identifying children for Rapid Catch-up

'It is essential that, by the end of their primary education, all pupils are able to read fluently, and with confidence, in any subject in their forthcoming secondary education.'
English National Curriculum (DfE, 2013)

Any child in your school who is reading at below the expected level for their age should be assessed immediately to identify what support and teaching they need to become fluent, accurate readers. For children in Reception or Year 1 who are following the Little Wandle programme, intervention should be in the form of Daily Keep-up. (See the Daily Keep-up area of the Little Wandle website.)

Using the assessment materials

Children in Year 2 and above who are not at age-related expectations for reading should be assessed using the Rapid Catch-up phonics assessment and fluency assessment to check if they need to follow the Little Wandle Rapid Catch-up programme. The assessments, assessment guidance and supporting videos can be found in the Rapid Catch-up area of the Little Wandle website, and you will find detailed information on how to carry out the assessments there.

We have also provided images and word cards for all of the assessment words to enable you to assess non-verbal children. Refer to the guidance documents for instructions on how to carry out these assessments.

By using the Rapid Catch-up assessments, you will be able to work out exactly what gaps these children have, and put in place a robust programme to ensure they learn to read quickly. The assessments will also help you to match children to the appropriate reading book.

You will need to:
- assess all children on entry to the Rapid Catch-up programme so their pathway and specific teaching can be created
- re-assess children when they complete Phases 2, 3 and 4
- assess children who are following the Phase 5 part of the programme every four weeks
- assess children at the end of the programme to check they are ready to leave Little Wandle Rapid Catch-up.

The Rapid Catch-up fluency assessment should be used to find out about children's reading accuracy and rate of reading as they become more confident readers in Phase 5, and to tell you whether children have gained enough fluency and accuracy to exit the Rapid Catch-up programme. In order to understand the meaning of what they are reading, children need to be reading at approximately 90 words per minute.

Pathways

The results of the initial Rapid Catch-up assessment will determine the correct pathway through the programme for each child.

Pathway 1: Some children will have large gaps in their knowledge and need to follow the whole Rapid Catch-up programme from the beginning. Other children will have secure knowledge of early phase GPCs but large gaps in later phases – these children will be able to start the programme part way through. For children with large gaps, teach all of the content in the weekly grids from the relevant point, using the lesson templates and prompt cards for support.

Pathway 2: Some children will have smaller gaps in their knowledge that can be filled in short, focused lessons. If you are filling in specific gaps for a child, as identified by the Rapid Catch-up assessment, use the prompt cards to guide your teaching and the words identified in the 'Word cards' column of the assessment in your lessons. You can also refer to the relevant parts of the weekly grids.

Your four-weekly assessments will enable you to check the children's progress and further tailor the programme for each child. You may decide to switch between the pathways. While the aim of the programme is to enable children to catch up and become readers quickly, it is important to ensure that the children have secure knowledge of all the GPCs and words in a phase before moving on.

Using initial assessment results to determine the correct pathway

Part 1: Phase 2
Assessment: 32 GPCs/15 words

Assessment results				Action
If **all GPCs**	and	at least **13 words**	are read automatically	reteach any incorrect words then move to Part 2: Phase 3 of the assessment
If **any GPCs**	or	**3 words** or more	are read incorrectly or not read	teach the whole programme from the beginning of Phase 2 (Pathway 1)

Part 2: Phase 3
Assessment: 14 GPCs/22 words

Assessment results				Action
If at least **12 GPCs**	and	at least **19 words**	are read automatically	reteach any incorrect GPCs and words then move to Part 3: Phase 4 of the assessment
If **3 to 4 GPCs**	or	**4 to 6 words**	are read incorrectly or not read	teach to the gaps (Pathway 2)
If **5 GPCs** or more	or	**7 words** or more	are read incorrectly or not read	teach the whole programme from the beginning of Phase 3 (Pathway 1)

Part 3: Phase 4
Assessment: 18 words

Assessment results	Action
If at least **16 words** are read correctly, **10** of which are read automatically	reteach any incorrect words then move to Part 4: Phase 5 of the assessment
If **3 to 4 words** are read incorrectly or not read, but at least **10 words** are read automatically	teach to the gaps (Pathway 2)
If **5 or more words** are read incorrectly or not read, and fewer than **10 words** are read automatically	teach the whole programme from the beginning of Phase 4 (Pathway 1)

Part 4: Phase 5
Assessment: 42 GPCs/92 words

Assessment results				Action
If at least **40 GPCs**	and	at least **87 words**	are read automatically	reteach any incorrect GPCs and words. These children do not need to follow Rapid Catch-up.
If **5 to 10 GPCs**	or	**6 to 15 words**	are read incorrectly or not read	teach to the gaps (Pathway 2)
If **11 GPCs** or more	or	**16 words** or more	are read incorrectly or not read	teach the whole programme from the beginning of Phase 5 (Pathway 1)

Common issues

Not blending at Phases 2 and 3: Check the children's oral blending skills using the oral blending assessments. Use teacher-led blending every day. See the guidance for 'Blending and reading words – super-supported method' on page 36.

Not reading words automatically: See the guidance for 'Reading words with/without overt blending' on page 45.

Not able to identify the digraphs/trigraphs in words: Go back to teacher-led blending using the grapheme cards. See also the guidance for 'Reading words with speedy digraph recognition' on page 44.

Incomplete knowledge of the alphabetic code: Children who have not fully understood the alphabetic code can often read common words by sight but struggle to read words in context with the same GPCs. If we don't teach these children how to read any word using their alphabetic knowledge, they will struggle to become fluent readers and access the curriculum. If children can read the assessment words but not read the GPCs or identify the GPCs in the words, they will need to follow the Phase 5 part of the programme.

Assessment of progress

You should use the assessment materials to carry out summative assessments at the end of Phases 2, 3 and 4. Children following the Phase 5 part of the programme need to be assessed at four-weekly intervals to ensure they are secure, and continue to be secure, in each Phase 5 set. The Phase 5 sets are highlighted on the Rapid Catch-up assessment teacher's mark and record sheet.

The timetable below sets out when assessments should take place for children completing the whole programme (Pathway 1). Children with smaller gaps who are following Pathway 2 should also be assessed at least once every four weeks to check on progress and to ensure they are on the correct pathway.

Providing additional challenge

If children following the Rapid Catch-up programme are not finding the pace and progression challenging enough but still need support to catch up with their peers, continue to follow the Rapid Catch-up programme but put a greater emphasis on practising spelling in words and sentences. You can use the words and sentences from the weekly grids. Ask the children to write their own sentences using words they have recently learned. You can also explore spelling patterns by comparing words and looking at where in a word a grapheme often appears: beginning, middle or end.

Adapting the pace

For some children, the pace of Rapid Catch-up can initially feel very fast, and they may need some time to gain confidence and get the basics right at a slower pace before returning to the expected pace of the programme. For other children, the pace of Rapid Catch-up will remain too fast and, for these children, we recommend that you adapt the pace of teaching for them so that they are successful. Refer to the guidance 'Rapid Catch-up: Adapted pace' on the Little Wandle website.

Exiting the programme

Children who have completed the programme, secured all of the Phase 5 GPCs and can read them with ease, and have a reading accuracy speed of 90+ words per minute are ready to exit the phonics instruction part of the Rapid Catch-up programme.

They will, however, need to continue reading practice sessions with the Phase 5 Set 5 7+ reading books. Reading these books will ensure that they are practising their phonic knowledge in context and will provide challenge in terms of vocabulary and comprehension. Continue to use the 'Grow the code' grapheme chart in class to aid spelling and ensure that the children are given time to use their phonic knowledge to decode new words when they are reading.

Organising and timetabling Rapid Catch-up

Typically, you will be teaching individual children in the Rapid Catch-up lessons but the programme can be used for small groups if the children have been assessed to have largely the same needs. All of the resources and activities in this guide can be used with individuals or groups of children. For simplicity we have used the term 'children' throughout.

In order for children to make rapid progress, Rapid Catch-up phonics lessons must be timetabled three times a week. The lessons on days 1 and 2 will take 20 minutes each. For day 3, you will need to timetable a 10-minute phonics lesson and a 10- to 15-minute reading practice session. (We recommend two short lessons/sessions but these could be combined if appropriate.) Lessons 4 and 5 will be short reading practice sessions of 10 to 15 minutes each.

The three reading practice sessions are essential so children have quality teaching of reading and time to apply their secure phonic knowledge in age-appropriate decodable books.

Day 1	20-minute phonics lesson
Day 2	20-minute phonics lesson
Day 3	Review day: A quick review of the teaching from days 1 and 2 10-minute phonics lesson plus 10- to 15-minute reading practice session. In Phases 2 and 3, you will use the blending practice books for this session.
Day 4	10- to 15-minute reading practice session
Day 5	10- to 15-minute reading practice session

Where the lessons should take place

Make sure you have a base for your Rapid Catch-up teaching, so the lessons are in a familiar place for the children. This will really help with storing and organising your resources, too. The room should be quiet and private; a corridor is not the right place for a child who needs to listen carefully and concentrate, and who may feel very vulnerable about their reading status. Privacy is really important as it will allow the child to relax and for you to create the right atmosphere for learning together.

Training

Rapid Catch-up teachers must be fully trained, in both the full initial Little Wandle training and the specific Rapid Catch-up training. All the training is available online and on-demand in the CPD area of the Little Wandle website.

Rapid Catch-up progression

The aim of the Rapid Catch-up programme is to rapidly teach children to read – there is no time to delay. Each day a child cannot read in class is a day that they needlessly struggle. This is why we have accelerated the teaching of each phase and created slimline lessons. Below is an overview of the GPCs and tricky words covered in each phase. The content for each lesson – including GPCs; words for blending, reading and spelling; tricky words; and sentences for reading and writing – is shown in the weekly grids (on the Little Wandle website).

Phase 2

Length of teaching: four weeks		
New GPCs covered	Week 1	s a t p i n m d
	Week 2	g o c k ck e u r h
	Week 3	b l ll f ff ss j v w y x z zz
	Week 4	qu ch sh th ng nk
Tricky words taught		and is I the as has his her put* pull* full* no go to into we me be he of she push* *depending on accent

Phase 3

Length of teaching: four weeks		
New GPCs covered	Week 1	ai ee igh oa oo ar
	Week 2	**oo** or ur ow oi ear
	Week 3	air er double letters
	Week 4	longer words and suffixes –ing and –es
Tricky words taught		was you they my by all are pure sure

Phase 4

Length of teaching: four weeks		
Word types covered	Week 1	Adjacent consonants with short vowels
	Week 2	Adjacent consonants with long vowels
	Week 3	Suffixes: –ed /t/, –ed /id/, –ed /d/, –ing, –er, –est
	Week 4	Two-syllable words with adjacent consonants Compound words and multi-syllable words with adjacent consonants
Tricky words taught		said so have like some come love do were here little says there when what one out today

Phase 5

Length of teaching: 14 weeks			
New GPCs covered	Week 1	/ai/ ay play /ow/ ou cloud /oi/ oy toy	/ee/ ea each /ur/ ir bird /oo/ ue blue /yoo/ ue rescue
	Week 2	/yoo/ u unicorn /igh/ ie pie /igh/ i tiger	/oa/ o go /ai/ a paper /ee/ e he
	Week 3	/oa/ o-e home /ai/ a-e shake /ee/ e-e these	/igh/ i-e time /oo/ /yoo/ u-e rude cute /oo/ /yoo/ ew chew new
	Week 4	/or/ aw claw /ee/ ie shield /ee/ y funny	/e/ ea head /w/ wh wheel /igh/ y fly
	Week 5	/oa/ oe toe /oa/ ou shoulder /oa/ ow snow	/j/ g giant /f/ ph phone /s/ c ice
	Week 6	/l/ le apple /l/ al metal /v/ ve give	/u/ o-e some /u/ o mother /u/ ou young
	Week 7	/z/ se cheese /s/ se mouse /s/ ce fence	/ee/ ey donkey /oo/ ui fruit /oo/ ou soup
	Week 8	/ur/ or word /oo/ u awful /oo/ oul could	/air/ are share /air/ ear bear /air/ ere there
	Week 9	/or/ au author /or/ aur dinosaur /or/ oor floor	/or/ al walk /or/ a water /ch/ tch match /ch/ ture adventure
	Week 10	/ar/ al half /ar/ a father* /o/ a want	/ur/ ear learn /r/ wr wrist /z/ ze freeze
	Week 11	/s/ st whistle /s/ sc science /c/ ch school /sh/ ch chef	schwa in longer words schwa at the end of words (-or, -our, -re, -a)
	Week 12	/ai/ eigh eight /ai/ aigh straight /ai/ ey grey /ai/ ea break	/n/ kn knee /n/ gn gnaw /m/ mb thumb
	Week 13	/ear/ ere here /ear/ eer deer /zh/ su treasure /zh/ si vision	/j/ dge bridge /j/ ge large /i/ y crystal
	Week 14	/sh/ ti potion /sh/ ssi mission /sh/ si mansion /sh/ ci delicious	/or/ augh daughter /or/ our your /or/ oar roar /or/ ore more
Tricky words taught	their people oh your Mr Mrs Ms ask could would should our house mouse water want again any many where who whole two school call different thought through friend work once laugh because eye busy beautiful pretty hour parents shoe move improve		

*depending on accent

Teaching Rapid Catch-up

There are many reasons why children may need Rapid Catch-up.

- They have missed chunks of schooling and so have gaps in their phonic knowledge.
- They have not been taught with consistency and so have not secured adequate phonic knowledge to read fluently.
- They need more practice and time to secure each stage of the phonic code and so have fallen behind their peers.
- They are new to the country and reading/speaking English.

Tone, praise and pace

Children who have not learned to read at the same time as their peers will have lost confidence and may show this through their behaviour. It is vital that we make them feel safe and ready to learn in their Rapid Catch-up lessons. Children may feel that they cannot learn to read, it is too difficult or not for them. It is up to you to help them believe that they can do this by showing them that it is possible and celebrating their successes.

Older children in particular need to feel that they are not being patronised or considered 'not intelligent' because they have not yet learned to read. We must make all our children feel that they **can** do this, that they are making progress in every lesson and that the end goal of reading is worth the effort.

Keep your tone warm and encouraging and the pace of the lesson brisk so that every moment is used to learn. This is valuable time that you have together – it is making a real difference to the children you work with. Try to see these lessons as a team effort with yourself and the children working together. This really does make a difference.

Keep cognitive load low

- Keep distractions to a minimum; only put out the resources that you need for the lesson.
- Don't talk too much – use the minimum talk needed to teach. Too much talk is overwhelming for some children.
- Use the Little Wandle teaching resources – the grapheme cards are linked to the grapheme charts and ensure consistency.
- Use the same routines and activities; consistency really helps children to focus on learning to read rather than learning to do a new activity.

Teaching support: lesson templates, weekly grids and prompt cards

The lesson templates for each phase (see pages 18 to 27) give you an overview of the Rapid Catch-up lesson. The weekly grids (on the Little Wandle website) detail the GPCs, words and tricky words that need to be taught or reviewed in each part of the lesson. The lesson content builds cumulatively, so it is important that you follow these in order.

The teaching in the Rapid Catch-up programme is pacy: this is vital because we want children to get back on track and reading as quickly as possible. But at times we need to slow down and drop the pace to ensure children secure new skills or knowledge. Our prompt cards (see pages 28 to 61) and 'How to' videos (on the Little Wandle website) will support you with this.

A word about the schwa

The schwa is the name for the most common sound in English. It is the unstressed sound that we find in many words; it makes an 'uh' sound, which varies according to accent. The phonemic symbol for the schwa sound is ə. Schwa can be represented in writing by all five vowels, and by a number of digraphs and trigraphs such as 'er', 'ou', 'or' and 'our'.

Introducing the schwa in Phase 3

Children first meet the schwa in Phase 3 when they read words ending in 'er'. In many accents the 'er' makes an unstressed vowel sound at the end of words such as 'bigger' and 'better', but in other accents these words are pronounced with pure sounds.

We also teach children to read multi-syllable words in Phase 3. Words such as 'hidden', 'lemon' and 'carrot' can be read using the GPCs the children know and with the chunking technique:

1) Say the word with pure sounds, a syllable at a time, for example: c-a-rr/o-t.

2) Tweak the pronunciation of the word 'but we say carrət' (with the schwa).

3) Teach vocabulary – 'a carrot is a yummy vegetable!'

The schwa in Phase 5

Many combinations of vowels can make the schwa sound, especially in longer words. In Phase 5 week 9 for example, we read the word 'adventure'. Here, we code 'ture' as ch – with a schwa at the end so it says /ch/ə!

In Phase 5 week 11, the (second) 'o' in 'crocodile', the 'u' in 'difficult', the 'a' in 'umbrella', the 'or' in 'actor' and the 're' in 'metre' can all make the schwa! Once again, it depends on accent. We teach children to read these words with the chunking method and pure sounds, and then how the word is said (in their accent) with the schwa. Always be guided by the children's accent and pronunciation. This is important as so many English words have the schwa.

Example words containing the schwa sound in Little Wandle Rapid Catch-up

Phase 3	Phase 4	Phase 5
bigger finger ladder carrot lemon	clearer further brighter children flower monster sunflower	annoy tiger paper feather giant octopus applaud water adventure* scissors parachute crocodile celebrate difficult actor flavour metre umbrella treasure vision magician

*coded as 'ture' /ch/ with a schwa at the end

How to use the resources

The physical teaching resources for Little Wandle Rapid Catch-up have been carefully created to help you teach with fidelity to the programme and use your assessment for learning to ensure all your children get the additional practice that they need to secure fluent reading of GPCs and words.

Grapheme cards

Use the **grapheme cards**:
- to teach each new GPC in Phases 2, 3 and 5. The Phase 2 and 3 grapheme cards are ideal to use when you are making the link between the grapheme, the phoneme and the mnemonic/catchphrase.
- to make the words used in teacher-led blending in Phase 2. This is a crucial part of our pedagogy and ensures that children are taught to blend step-by-step. In this way, we model how to blend in every Phase 2 lesson, until the children are secure and do not need this support anymore. You can see this in practice in the Rapid Catch-up 'How to' video 'Teacher-led blending'.

Use grapheme cards for teacher-led blending

- When reviewing GPCs: **Shuffle time**. Remember to use the grapheme side; only use the mnemonic/catchphrase if the children cannot automatically read the grapheme.
- For **Change it**. This game is part of the lessons in Phases 2, 3 and 4. You can see this in practice in the Rapid Catch-up 'How to' video 'Change it'.
- For **Mix it up**. Use the small grapheme cards to model spelling and for children to spell words in this one-to-one activity. You can see the activity in practice in the Rapid Catch-up 'How to' video 'Mix it up'.

Tip: A pocket chart or stand is very useful. Make sure you have all your graphemes in order, so you can make the changes easily!

The **grapheme cards for Phase 5** do not have an image or catchphrase. This is because we want the children to focus on learning to read the GPC and not on learning a catchphrase for each alternative pronunciation of a grapheme. Instead, we refer back to the Phase 2 or 3 GPC, as that is the image associated with that phoneme on all our resources, including the 'Grow the code' chart and map. This is how we create a visual schema for children to grow the complex alphabetic code.

Grapheme mats

Download the **grapheme mat** for Phases 2 and 3 and the 'Grow the code' grapheme mat from the Little Wandle website, to use with the children in the lessons.

Picture cards

Use the **picture cards** when introducing a new GPC in Phase 2. The picture card is the same image as the mnemonic, to maximise on the link between the phoneme, the mnemonic and the grapheme.

Rapid Catch-up word cards

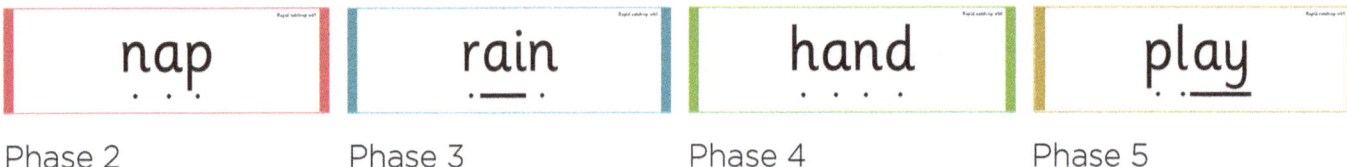

Phase 2 Phase 3 Phase 4 Phase 5

- Use the **Rapid Catch-up word cards** for independent reading. (This is in addition to teaching teacher-led blending with grapheme cards in Phase 2.)
- There are word cards for every phase. They are double sided with sound buttons on one side and just the word on the other.
- The word cards have coloured panels on the side to indicate the phase in which they are taught/reviewed: magenta for Phase 2, teal for Phase 3, green for Phase 4 and mustard for Phase 5. They also have the week they are taught/reviewed in the top right-hand corner to help with organisation.
- Additional copies of words reviewed in a different week are included, so you have all the words needed for each week.

Tricky word cards

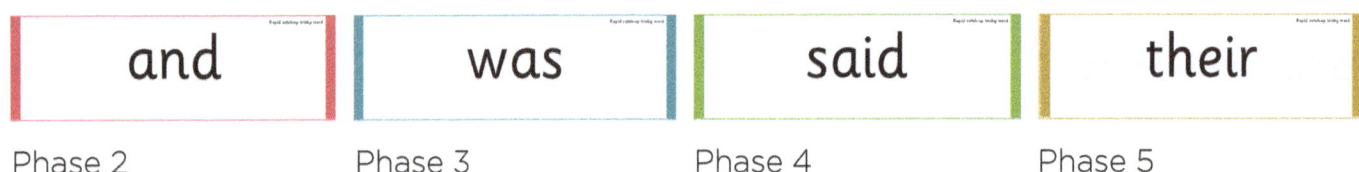

Phase 2 Phase 3 Phase 4 Phase 5

There are tricky word cards for every phase. They are single sided and do not have sound buttons. These are reviewed after they are taught so it is best to keep them together so it is easy to find the cards you want for any lesson.

The tricky word cards also have coloured panels on the side to indicate their phase.

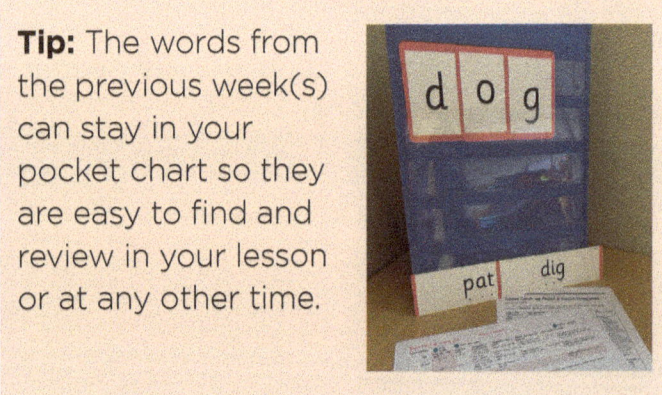

Tip: The words from the previous week(s) can stay in your pocket chart so they are easy to find and review in your lesson or at any other time.

How we chose the words

There are approximately 900 words/tricky words taught in the Rapid Catch-up programme. These are made up of the words used for oral and teacher-led blending, the words on the word cards and tricky word cards, plus additional words used in activities such as **Change it** and **Match the words to the pictures**.

Decodable words

We chose the words for the Rapid Catch-up programme carefully, using the original research from the 2007 Letters and Sounds[1], which identified the 300 most common words, and the Collins Corpus, which extracted the most frequent words from 1.2 million words in 950 titles aimed at children aged three to 11. In this way we could teach children to read words that would have the greatest impact on their reading as efficiently as possible. We have organised these words into a cumulative progression.

Tricky words

The tricky words remain the same as those in the core Little Wandle programme. They are the original tricky words from Letters and Sounds combined with the Common Exception Words from the English National Curriculum Year 1 and 2 Spelling appendix.

Fully decodable books

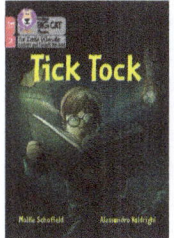   

Collins has created fully **decodable books** that exactly match the progression and ambition of our Rapid Catch-up programme. They have been written for children age 7+ and provide practice at the correct level for each phase as well as ensuring that children's vocabulary and language development is supported.

Use the Rapid Catch-up matching grid on the Little Wandle website to match each child's secure phonic knowledge in reading to the appropriate decodable reading book for the next four weeks.

Blending practice books

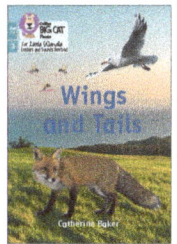   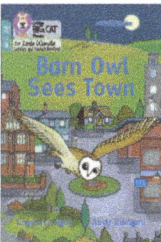

Among the decodable books are blending practice books for use in Phases 2, 3 and 4. These books have a very limited number of words and practise specific GPCs and word types. They are used to focus on blending skills and extending vocabulary. There are supporting teacher's notes to guide you through how to use them. You can also see these books being taught in the Rapid Catch-up 'How to' video 'Blending practice books'.

[1] *Masterson, J., Stuart, M., Dixon, M. and Lovejoy, S. (2003) Children's Printed Word Database: Economic and Social Research Council funded project, R00023406*

Lesson templates

Phase 2 template: Lessons 1 and 2

You will need: Phase 2 grapheme cards, picture cards, word cards, tricky word cards, images for **Match the words to the pictures** (from the website).

Quick review: GPCs and tricky words	Teach and practise: Teach new GPCs and words	Practise and apply

GPCs
• Ask the children to read speedy sounds.
• Use all cards – **grapheme side only**. (Only show the mnemonic side if the children are unsure.)
• Shuffle. Repeat.
 	
Tricky words
For each word:
• Ask the children to recall the 'tricky bit'. Take feedback.
• Ask the children to read the word
• Shuffle. Repeat.
	Phoneme
	• Introduce the new phoneme.
	• Teach pronunciation.
	• Use the **copy me method** to practise pronunciation. Repeat.
	
	Link to the picture card
	• Show the children the picture card for the grapheme.
	• Emphasise the initial/end phoneme of the word.
	
	Grapheme
	• Use the **copy me method** as you say the phoneme and draw your finger around the grapheme in the mnemonic (e.g. d d d duck). Repeat.
	• Use the **copy me method** as you show the grapheme, draw your finger around the grapheme and say its sound. Repeat several times.
	• Play the **Grapheme game**: Show alternate sides of the card as the children call out. Repeat several times.
	• Add the new grapheme card to the review pack. Play **Grapheme spotter** with the new GPC (see page 32).
	
	Oral blending
	• Use the **copy me method** to blend three words.
	• Ensure the children understand the meaning of each new word.
	
	Teacher-led blending
	• Use the grapheme cards to make the words. For each word:
	  • Model: Read and point to each grapheme. Sweep and blend.
	  • Use the **copy me method** to repeat the process with the children.
	  • Check and read each word together, giving less support. Watch and assess the children.
	
	Once the children can blend without support, use independent reading words.
	
	Independent reading
	• Use the word cards.
	• Show the word.
	• Point to each grapheme and then sweep to indicate blending. Do NOT help the children.
	• Look at the children (not the cards) and assess.
	• Read the word together.
	• Use pictures, props and simple definitions to ensure the children understand the meaning of each new word. (Some definitions and example sentences are provided in the grids.)
	
	New tricky words
	• Show the tricky word on the card.
	• Read the graphemes the children know.
	• Identify the tricky grapheme (in bold on the grid).
	• Read the tricky word.
	• Ask the children to read the tricky word with you.
	• Ask the children to read the tricky word independently.
		Change it
		• Make each word using the grapheme cards.
		• Point to each grapheme and then sweep to indicate blending. Do NOT help the children.
		• Look at the children (not the cards) and assess.
		• Model reading the word.
		• Change one grapheme in the word (see the grid for order) and repeat.
		
		Match the words to the pictures
		• Display the numbered pictures.
		• For each word:
		  • Ask the children to identify the digraphs. Take feedback.
		  • Ask the children to read the word.
		  • Ask them to tell you which picture matches the word by holding up the appropriate number of fingers.

Phase 2 template: Lesson 3 – Review

You will need: Phase 2 grapheme cards, word cards, tricky word cards, precision teaching grids (completed in advance of the lesson – see page 70), blending practice books, mini whiteboards and pens.

Quick review: GPCs and tricky words	Teach and practise: Precision teaching of GPCs and words	Practise and apply

Choose GPCs and tricky words from days 1 and 2.
 	
GPCs
• Ask the children to read speedy sounds.
• Use grapheme cards – **grapheme side only**. (Only show the mnemonic side if the children are unsure).
 	
Quick review
Shuffle. Repeat.
 	
Tricky words
For each word:
• Ask the children to recall the 'tricky bit'. Take feedback.
• Ask the children to read the word.
• Shuffle. Repeat.
	Precision teaching words
	In advance of the lesson, choose words from days 1 and 2 that need additional practice. Write the words in a random order on a copy of the precision teaching grids. Make a copy of the grid for each child.
	
	• Give each child a copy of the grid.
	• Choose a word, point to it on your grid – making sure that the children can see clearly as you point – and ask the children to read the word.
	• Ask the children to find the same word in their grid, point to it and read.
	• Now ask the children to read all the words in each line as they point.
	• If the children cannot read a word, model reading it and then ask them to repeat and continue.
	• Repeat, building on fluency.
	
	You can also use this activity to precision teach graphemes and tricky words if needed.
		Blending practice book
		Use the notes in the book to guide you. Use the blending practice book prompt cards (pages 54 to 55) and watch the 'How to' videos for further support.
		
		Mix it up (spelling with grapheme cards)*
		Display the grapheme cards you need to spell the word, as well as some extra grapheme cards as distractors.
		• Use the **copy me method** to say the word and then segment it.
		• Count the sounds in the word.
		• Model spelling the word:
		  • Segment the word and choose the correct grapheme for the first sound.
		  • Place the card on the table.
		  • Continue with all the sounds until you have spelled the word.
		  • Read the word.
		• Mix up the cards and ask the child to spell the word independently by segmenting and choosing the correct graphemes.
		• Ask the child to read the word.
		
		Spelling*
		• Use the **copy me method** to:
		  • Say the word.
		  • Segment it.
		  • Segment and count the sounds.
		• Model spelling the word.
		  • Say the word and how many sounds you need to spell it.
		  • Write each grapheme.
		  • Hide the word.
		• Ask the children to spell the word.
		• Check the word together.
		• Ask the children to check and correct their spelling.
		• Repeat for the other words.

*Choose either **Mix it up** (for one-to-one sessions) or **Spelling** (for one-to-one or groups) – whichever is appropriate for the child/children.

Phase 3 template: Lessons 1 and 2

You will need: Phase 3 grapheme cards, word cards, tricky word cards, images for **Match the words to the pictures** (from the website), blending practice books, mini whiteboards and pens.

Quick review: GPCs and tricky words	Teach and practise: Teach new GPCs and words	Practise and apply

GPCs
• Use grapheme cards – **grapheme side only**. (Only show the mnemonic side if the children are unsure).
• Ask the children to read speedy sounds.
• Shuffle. Repeat.
 	
Words
• Ask the children to identify the digraphs. Take feedback.
• Point and sweep to indicate blending.
• Chunk longer words.
• Shuffle. Ask the children to read without blending.
 	
Tricky words
For each word:
• Ask the children to recall the 'tricky bit'. Take feedback.
• Ask the children to read the word.
• Shuffle. Repeat.
	Phoneme
	• Introduce the new phoneme.
	• Teach pronunciation.
	• Use the **copy me method** to practise pronunciation. Repeat.
	
	Grapheme
	• Show the grapheme side of the grapheme card.
	• Use the mantra *'two letters, one sound'* and then say the sound.
	• Use the **copy me method** as you show the grapheme, draw your finger around the grapheme and say its sound. Repeat several times.
	• Show the catchphrase side of the grapheme card.
	• Teach the catchphrase.
	• Repeat several times.
	• Play the **Grapheme game**: Show alternate sides of the card as the children call out. Repeat several times.
	• Add the new grapheme card to the review pack. Play **Grapheme spotter** with the new GPC.
	
	Oral blending
	• Use the **copy me method** to blend three words. Ensure the children understand the meaning of each new word.
	
	Once the children can blend without support use independent reading words.
	
	Independent reading
	• Use the word cards.
	• Show the word.
	• Point to each grapheme and then sweep to indicate blending. Do NOT help the children.
	• Look at the children (not the cards) and assess.
	• Read the word together.
	• Use pictures, props and simple definitions to ensure the children understand the meaning of each new word. (Some definitions and example sentences are provided in the grids.)
	
	New tricky words
	• Show the tricky word on the card.
	• Read the graphemes the children know.
	• Identify the tricky grapheme (in bold on the grid).
	• Read the tricky word.
	• Ask the children to read the tricky word with you.
	• Ask the children to read the tricky word independently.
		Blending practice book
		Use the notes in the book to guide you.
		
		Mix it up (spelling with grapheme cards)*
		Display the grapheme cards you need to spell the word, as well as some extra grapheme cards as distractors.
		• Use the **copy me method** to say the word and then segment it.
		• Count the sounds in the word.
		• Model spelling the word:
		  • Segment the word and choose the correct grapheme for the first sound.
		  • Place the card on the table.
		  • Continue with all the sounds until you have spelled the word. Read the word.
		• Mix up the cards and ask the child to spell the word independently by segmenting and choosing the correct graphemes.
		• Ask the child to read the word.
		
		Spelling*
		• Use the **copy me method** to:
		  • Say the word.
		  • Segment it.
		  • Segment and count the sounds.
		• Model spelling the word.
		  • Say the word and how many sounds you need to spell it.
		  • Write each grapheme.
		  • Hide the word.
		• Ask the children to spell the word.
		• Check the word together.
		• Ask the children to check and correct their spelling.
		• Repeat for the other words.
		
		Spelling tricky words
		• Use the same method as above, identifying the 'tricky bit' as you spell it.
		
		Change it
		• Make each word using the grapheme cards.
		• Point to each grapheme and then sweep to indicate blending. Do NOT help the children.
		• Look at the children (not the cards) and assess.
		• Model reading the word.
		• Change one grapheme in the word (see the grid for order) and repeat.
		
		Match the words to the pictures
		See page 21.

*Choose either **Mix it up** (for one-to-one sessions) or **Spelling** (for one-to-one or groups) – whichever is appropriate.

Phase 3 template: Lesson 3 – Review

You will need: Phase 2 and 3 grapheme cards, word cards, tricky word cards, precision teaching grids (completed in advance of the lesson – see page 70), images for **Match the words to the pictures** (from the website), blending practice books, mini whiteboards and pens.

Quick review: GPCs and tricky words	Teach and practise: Precision teaching of GPCs and words	Practise and apply

Choose GPCs, words and tricky words from days 1 and 2.
 	
GPCs
Use grapheme cards – **grapheme side only**. (Only show the catchphrase side if the children are unsure).
• Ask the children to read speedy sounds.
• Shuffle. Repeat.
 	
Words
• Ask the children to identify the digraphs. Take feedback.
• Point and sweep to indicate blending.
• Chunk longer words.
• Shuffle. Ask the children to read without blending.
 	
Tricky words
For each word:
• Ask the children to recall the 'tricky bit'. Take feedback.
• Ask the children to read the word.
• Shuffle. Repeat.
	Precision teaching words
	In advance of the lesson, choose words from days 1 and 2 that need additional practice. Write the words in a random order on a copy of the precision teaching grids.
	
	• Put the filled-in grid in front of the children.
	• Choose a word, point to it and ask the children to read it.
	• Ask the children to find the same word in the grid, point to it and read.
	• Now ask the children to read all the words in each line as they point.
	• If the children cannot read a word, model reading it and then ask them to repeat and continue.
	• Repeat, building on fluency.
	
	You can also use this activity to precision teach graphemes and tricky words if needed.
		Blending practice book
		Use the notes in the book to guide you. Use the blending practice book prompt cards (pages 54 to 55) and watch the 'How to' videos for further support.
		
		Match the words to the pictures
		• Display the numbered pictures.
		• For each word:
		  • Ask the children to identify the digraphs. Take feedback.
		  • Ask the children to read the word.
		  • Ask them to tell you which picture matches the word by holding up the appropriate finger.

Phase 4 template: Lessons 1 and 2

You will need: Phase 4 word cards, tricky word cards, grapheme cards, images for **Match the words to the pictures** (from the website), the sentences for **Read the sentence** written on a flipchart or large piece of paper (or from the website), mini whiteboards and pens.

Quick review: Words and tricky words	Teach and practise: Teach new words	Practise and apply

Words
• Ask the children to identify the digraphs. Take feedback.
• Point and sweep to indicate blending.
• Chunk longer words.
• Shuffle. Ask the children to read without blending.
 	
Tricky words
For each word:
• Ask the children to recall the 'tricky bit'. Take feedback.
• Ask the children to read the word.
• Shuffle. Repeat.
	Oral blending
	Use the **copy me method** to blend three words. Ensure the children understand the meaning of each new word.
	
	Once the children can blend without support use independent reading words.
	
	Independent reading
	Use the word cards. For each word:
	• Show the word.
	• Point to each grapheme and then sweep to indicate blending. Do NOT help the children.
	• Look at the children (not the cards) and assess.
	• Read the word together.
	• Use pictures, props and simple definitions to ensure the children understand the meaning of each new word. (Some definitions and example sentences are provided in the grids.)
	
	New tricky words
	• Show the tricky word on the card.
	• Read the graphemes the children know.
	• Identify the tricky grapheme (in bold on the grid).
	• Read the tricky word.
	• Ask the children to read the tricky word with you.
	• Ask the children to read the tricky word independently.
		Change it
		Make each word using the grapheme cards.
		• Point to each grapheme and then sweep to indicate blending. Do NOT help the children.
		• Look at the children (not the cards) and assess.
		• Model reading the word.
		• Change one grapheme in the word (see the grid for order) and repeat.
		
		Match the words to the pictures
		Display the numbered pictures.
		For each word:
		• Ask the children to identify the digraphs. Take feedback.
		• Ask the children to read the word.
		• Ask them to tell you which picture matches the word by holding up the appropriate number of fingers.
		
		Spell a tricky word
		• Use the **copy me method** to:
		  • Say the word.
		  • Segment it.
		  • Segment and count the sounds.
		  • Model spelling the word.
		• Say the word and how many sounds you need to spell it.
		• Write each grapheme, pointing out the 'tricky bit'.
		• Hide the word.
		• Ask the children to spell the word.
		• Check the word together.
		• Ask the children to check and correct their spelling.
		• Repeat for the other words.
		
		Read the sentence
		Ask the children to read aloud as you point to the words.
		• Read the sentence together.
		• Tell the children to read the sentence one more time.

Quick review: Words and tricky words	Teach and practise: Teach new words	Practise and apply

(See previous page)	(See previous page)	**Mix it up (spelling with grapheme cards)***
		Display the grapheme cards you need to spell the word, as well as some extra grapheme cards as distractors.
		• Use the **copy me method** to say the word and then segment it.
		• Count the sounds in the word.
		• Model spelling the word:
		  • Segment the word and choose the correct grapheme for the first sound.
		  • Place the card on the table.
		  • Continue with all the sounds until you have spelled the word.
		  • Read the word.
		• Mix up the cards and ask the child to spell the word independently by segmenting and choosing the correct graphemes.
		• Ask the child to read the word.
		
		Spelling*
		• Use the **copy me method** to:
		  • Say the word.
		  • Segment it.
		  • Segment and count the sounds.
		• Model spelling the word.
		  • Say the word and how many sounds you need to spell it.
		  • Write each grapheme.
		  • Hide the word.
		• Ask the children to spell the word.
		• Check the word together.
		• Ask the children to check and correct their spelling.
		• Repeat for the other words.

*Choose either **Mix it up** (for one-to-one sessions) or **Spelling** (for one-to-one or groups) – whichever is appropriate for the child/children.

Phase 4 template: Lesson 3 – Review

You will need: Phase 4 word cards, tricky word cards, grapheme cards, precision teaching grids (completed in advance of the lesson – see page 70), decodable books, images for **Match the words to the pictures** (from the website), mini whiteboards and pens.

Quick review: Words and tricky words	Teach and practise: Precision teaching of words	Practise and apply

Words
• Ask the children to identify the digraphs. Take feedback.
• Point and sweep to indicate blending.
• Chunk longer words.
• Shuffle. Ask the children to read without blending.
 	
Tricky words
For each word:
• Ask the children to recall the 'tricky bit'. Take feedback.
• Ask the children to read the word.
• Shuffle. Repeat.
	Precision teaching words
	In advance of the lesson, choose words from days 1 and 2 that need additional practice. Write the words in a random order on a copy of the precision teaching grids. Make a copy of the grid for each child.
	
	• Give each child a copy of the grid.
	• Choose a word, point to it on your grid – making sure that the children can see clearly as you point – and ask the children to read the word.
	• Ask the children to find the same word in their grid, point to it and read.
	• Now ask the children to read all the words in each line as they point.
	• If the children cannot read a word, model reading it and then ask them to repeat and continue.
	• Repeat, building on fluency.
	
	You can also use this activity to precision teach graphemes and tricky words if needed.
		Reading book
		Use the notes in the book to guide you. Use the reading practice session prompt cards (pages 56 to 61) and 'How to' videos for further support.
		
		Match the words to the pictures*
		Display the numbered pictures. For each word:
		• Ask the children to identify the digraphs. Take feedback.
		• Ask the children to read the word.
		• Ask them to tell you which picture matches the word by holding up the appropriate finger.
		
		Mix it up (spelling with grapheme cards)/ Spelling**
		• See page 23.
		
		Write the sentence
		Prepare:
		• Say the sentence.
		• Use the **copy me method** to practise saying the sentence until the children are confident.
		• Write the sentence. Model how you:
		  • use capital letters and punctuation
		  • segment to spell
		  • remember digraphs/trigraphs
		  • remember the 'tricky bit' of tricky words.
		• Hide the sentence.
		Write:
		• Ask the children to write the sentence.
		• Check the sentence together.
		• Ask the children to check and correct their spelling.

*The weekly grids will have one activity either **Write the sentence** or **Match the words to the pictures**.
Choose either **Mix it up (for one-to-one sessions) or **Spelling** (for one-to-one or groups) – whichever is appropriate for the child/children.

Phase 5 template: Lessons 1 and 2

You will need: Phase 5 grapheme cards, word cards, tricky word cards, the sentences for **Read the sentence** written on a flipchart or large piece of paper (or from the website), mini whiteboards and pens, images for **Sort the words by grapheme/phoneme** (from the website), 'Grow the code' chart or mats.

Quick review: GPCs, words and tricky words	Teach and practise: Teach new GPCs and words	Practise and apply

GPCs
• Use grapheme cards.
• Ask the children to read speedy sounds.
• Quick review:
• Shuffle. Repeat.
 	
Words
• Ask the children to identify the digraphs. Take feedback.
• Point and sweep to indicate blending.
• Chunk longer words.
• Shuffle. Ask the children to read without blending.
 	
Tricky words
For each word:
• Ask the children to recall the 'tricky bit'. Take feedback.
• Ask the children to read the word.
• Shuffle. Repeat.
	Grapheme
	Introduce the new GPC.
	• Use the **copy me method** to practise pronunciation. Repeat.
	• Show linking graphemes for the new sound (in bold on the planning grid).
	• Show the new grapheme card.
	• Ask the children to read the grapheme – hide and show. Repeat.
	• Add the new grapheme card to the review pack.
	• Play **Grapheme spotter** with the new GPC.
	
	Oral blending
	Use the **copy me method** to blend three words. Ensure the children understand the meaning of each new word.
	
	Once the children can blend without support, use independent reading words.
	
	Independent reading
	Use the word cards. For each word:
	• Show the word.
	• Point to each grapheme and then sweep to indicate blending. Do NOT help the children.
	• Look at the children (not the cards) and assess.
	• Read the word together.
	• Use pictures, props and simple definitions to ensure the children understand the meaning of each new word. (Some definitions and example sentences are provided in the grids.)
	
	New tricky words
	• Show the tricky word on the card.
	• Read the graphemes the children know.
	• Identify the tricky grapheme (in bold on the grid).
	• Read the tricky word.
	• Ask the children to read the tricky word with you.
	• Ask the children to read the tricky word independently.
		Read the sentence
		• Ask the children to read aloud as you point to the words.
		• Read the sentence together.
		• Tell the children to read the sentence one more time.
		
		Write the sentence
		Prepare:
		• Say the sentence.
		• Use the **copy me method** to practise saying the sentence until the children are confident.
		• Write the sentence. Model how you:
		  • use capital letters and punctuation
		  • segment to spell
		  • remember digraphs/trigraphs
		  • remember the 'tricky bit' of tricky words.
		• Hide the sentence.
		Write:
		• Ask the children to write the sentence.
		• Check the sentence together.
		• Ask the children to check and correct their spelling.
		
		Mix it up (spelling with grapheme cards)*
		Display the grapheme cards you need to spell the word, as well as some extra grapheme cards as distractors.
		• Use the **copy me method** to say the word and then segment it.
		• Count the sounds in the word.
		• Model spelling the word:
		  • Segment the word and choose the correct grapheme for the first sound.
		  • Place the card on the table.
		  • Continue with all the sounds until you have spelled the word.
		  • Read the word.
		• Mix up the cards and ask the child to spell the word independently by segmenting and choosing the correct graphemes.
		• Ask the child to read the word.

Quick review: GPCs, words and tricky words	Teach and practise: Teach new GPCs and words	Practise and apply

(See previous page)	(See previous page)	**Spelling***
		• Use the **copy me method** to:
		  • Say the word.
		  • Segment it.
		  • Segment and count the sounds.
		• Model spelling the word.
		  • Say the word and how many sounds you need to spell it.
		  • Write each grapheme.
		  • Hide the word.
		• Ask the children to spell the word.
		• Check the word together.
		• Ask the children to check and correct their spelling.
		• Repeat for the other words.
		
		Spell a tricky word
		Use the same method as **Spelling** (above), identifying the 'tricky bit' as you spell it.
		
		Change it
		• Make each word using the grapheme cards.
		• Point to each grapheme and then sweep to indicate blending. Do NOT help the children.
		• Look at the children (not the cards) and assess.
		• Model reading the word.
		• Change one grapheme in the word (see the grid for order) and repeat.
		
		Sort the words by grapheme/phoneme
		• Tell the children that they are sorting the words they read by the two different graphemes/phonemes.
		• Use an image for each grapheme/phoneme (available on the website).
		• Ask the children to read each word.
		• Ask them to put the word by the image showing the correct grapheme/phoneme.
		
		Grow the code
		• Show the children the grapheme card for the day's GPC.
		• Find the new grapheme on the 'Grow the code' chart and review any linking graphemes.
		• Ask the children to write down as many different spellings of that day's 'Grow the code' phoneme as they know.
		• Take feedback.
		• Show the children the 'Grow the code' GPCs – did they get them all?

*Choose either **Mix it up** (for one-to-one sessions) or **Spelling** (for one-to-one or groups) – whichever is appropriate for the child/children.

Phase 5 template: Lesson 3 – Review

You will need: Phase 5 grapheme cards, word cards, tricky word cards, precision teaching grids (completed in advance of the lesson – see page 70), images for **Match the words to the pictures** (from the website), decodable books.

Quick review: GPCs, words and tricky words	Teach and practise: Precision teaching of GPCs and words	Practise and apply
Use GPCs, words and tricky words from days 1 and 2. **GPCs** • Use grapheme cards. • Ask the children to read speedy sounds. • Shuffle. Repeat. **Words** • Ask the children to identify the digraphs. Take feedback. • Point and sweep to indicate blending. • Chunk longer words. • Shuffle. Ask the children to read without blending. **Tricky words** For each word: • Ask the children to recall the 'tricky bit'. Take feedback. • Ask the children to read the word. • Shuffle. Repeat.	**Precision teaching words** In advance of the lesson, choose words from days 1 and 2 that need additional practice. Write the words in a random order on a copy of the precision teaching grids. Make a copy of the grid for each child. • Give each child a copy of the grid. • Choose a word, point to it on your grid – making sure that the children can see clearly as you point – and ask the children to read the word. • Ask the children to find the same word in their grid, point to it and read. • Now ask the children to read all the words in each line as they point. • If the children cannot read a word, model reading it and then ask them to repeat and continue. • Repeat, building on fluency. You can also use this activity to precision teach graphemes and tricky words if needed.	**Match the words to the pictures** Display the numbered pictures. For each word: • Ask the children to identify the digraphs. Take feedback. • Ask the children to read the word. • Ask them to tell you which picture matches the word by holding up the appropriate finger. **Reading book** Use the notes in the book to guide you. Use the reading practice session prompt cards (pages 56 to 61) and 'How to' videos for further support.

Reading practice sessions: Guidance for reading practice sessions is included in the prompt cards on pages 54 to 61.

Prompt cards and 'How to' videos

The teaching in the Rapid Catch-up programme is pacy and this is vital because we want children to get back on track and reading as quickly as possible. But there are times when we need to slow down and drop the pace to ensure children secure new skills or knowledge.

The **prompt cards** have been created to detail a small-step approach to the teaching of each aspect of Rapid Catch-up. Use them in one-to-one teaching sessions when children need additional support in order to secure a skill. The prompt cards give you all the steps and scaffolds you could need but you may find that your children do not need every scaffold. Once the skill has been secured, you can return to the main Rapid Catch-up lesson plans and its quicker pace of teaching. Ensure you are still teaching to the point of challenge – remember every lesson is precious and a chance to help our children get closer to becoming fluent readers!

The 'How to' videos feature children who are on the Rapid Catch-up programme so at times there are fewer scaffolds based on their needs.

There are prompt cards and accompanying 'How to' videos covering the following:

For phonics lessons:

Quick review	**Page**
All phases: GPCs	30
Phases 3 to 5: Words	30
All phases: Tricky words	31

Teach and practise	
Phase 2: Teaching a new GPC	32
Phases 2 and 3: Teaching a digraph/trigraph	33
Phase 5: Teaching a new GPC and oral blending	34
Phases 2, 3 and 4: Oral blending	35
Phase 2: Blending and reading words – super-supported method	36
Phase 2: Blending and reading words – supported method	37
Phase 2: Blending and reading words – whisper method	38
Phase 2: Blending and reading words – independent reading	39
Phases 3 and 5: Reading words	40
All phases: Reading words ending with –s and –es	41
All phases: Reading tricky words	42
All phases: Reading longer words	43
All phases: Reading words with speedy digraph recognition	44

All phases: Reading words with/without overt blending	45
Phase 4: Reading words with adjacent consonants	46
Phase 5: Reading words with graphemes that have more than one sound	47
Phase 5: Reading words containing a split vowel digraph	48

Practise and apply

Phase 5: Grow the code	49
All phases: Change it	49
All phases: Match the words to the pictures	49
All phases: Mix it up (spelling with grapheme cards)	50
All phases: Spelling (without grapheme cards)	50
All phases: Spelling tricky words	51
Phase 5: Sort the words by grapheme/phoneme	51
Phases 4 and 5: Read the sentence	52
Phases 4 and 5: Write the sentence	52

Review lesson

All phases: Precision teaching	53

For reading practice sessions:

Phases 2, 3 and 4: Reading blending practice books	54
All phases: Reading the 7+ books – decoding	56
All phases: Reading the 7+ books – prosody	58
All phases: Reading the 7+ books – comprehension	61

Prompt cards: Quick review

All phases: GPCs

You will need: Grapheme cards for the GPCs highlighted in the 'Quick review' column of the planning grid.

What to do	Notes

• **Say:** *Let's read our speedy sounds.*
• Show each grapheme card at a consistent pace to ensure quick recognition of sounds.
• Look at the children (not at the cards) to assess their reading.
• Do not read or mouth the sounds to the children.
• Shuffle the cards and repeat.
	• Ensure good flashcard control:
	  • Take care to turn the cards at a fairly rapid pace.
	  • Hold the cards at the edge.
	  • Ensure the cards are at a height that is easy for the children to see.
	• Pay close attention to the children at risk of falling behind, to ensure good participation.
	• In Phases 2 and 3, only show the mnemonic/catchphrase side if the children are unsure.
	• At this and every subsequent stage, take note of any children who are struggling, and make sure they get additional practice, either within the Rapid Catch-up lesson or at another time during the day.

Phases 3 to 5: Words

You will need: Word cards for the words highlighted in the 'Quick review' column of the planning grid.

What to do	Notes
Read words • **Say:** *Let's read some words we have read before.* • Show the word. • Ask the children to identify the digraphs/trigraphs. Take feedback. • Point to each letter and sweep, to signal to the children to read each sound and blend. • Repeat the procedure with the other review words. **Quick review** • Shuffle the cards. • Tell the children to read the words without sounding out. Remind them this means blending in their heads. • Show each card and sweep beneath the word to signal blending. • Shuffle again, asking the children to read at a quicker pace this time. • Ensure there is enough time for the children to read each word. • Look at the children (not at the cards) to assess their reading and readiness to blend. • Model reading the word and then give a contextualising sentence or definition, if needed. • Repeat the procedure with the other review words.	• As the words are all review words, display them without sound buttons. • Use minimal language to ensure the children can focus on the reading of the words. • Pointing out the digraphs/trigraphs should be pacy. • Watch the children carefully to ensure they are blending in their heads. (Children will often mouth the sounds to themselves at this stage.) • Encourage the children to indicate – with a silent gesture (e.g. nodding their head, thumbs up) – when they are ready to blend. • Provide additional blending practice for children who are struggling to blend (see the prompt cards on pages 36 to 39).

All phases: Tricky words

You will need: Tricky word cards for the words highlighted in the 'Quick review' column of the planning grid.

What to do	Notes
<ul><li>Tell the children you want them to read the words quickly.</li><li>Show each card.</li><li>Ensure there is enough time for the children to read each word.</li><li>Shuffle again, asking the children to read at a quicker pace this time.</li><li>Look at the children (not at the cards) to assess their reading.</li></ul>	<ul><li>Ideally, the children will read these words quickly and commit them to their long-term memory (orthographic store).</li><li>If the children cannot read a tricky word, identify the 'tricky bit' by pointing to the tricky grapheme and saying its sound.</li></ul>

Prompt cards: Teach and practise

Phase 2: Teaching a new GPC

You will need: Grapheme card and picture card for the GPC you are teaching.

What to do	Notes
Phoneme • Introduce the new phoneme. • Model the correct enunciation of the phoneme a few times. Ensure the children can see how you make the sound. • Use the **copy me method** to get the children to practise saying the phoneme after you, several times. • Use the picture card: 　• Show the children the picture card for the grapheme. 　• Emphasise the initial/end phoneme of the word. 　• Use **copy me** so the children say the sound and then the name of the object.	• Ensure you use a clear voice. • You may need to exaggerate your mouth movements to help the children really 'see' how to make the sound. • Use the picture card for the GPC you are teaching. • Graphemes at the end of words are 'x', 'ck', 'll', 'ff', 'ss', 'zz', 'sh', 'th', 'ng' and 'nk'. • You can find guidance for pronouncing the Phase 2 sounds on page 62 and on the Little Wandle website.
Grapheme • Show the mnemonic side of the grapheme card. • Draw the letter formation over the picture as you say the sound – saying the mnemonic at the end of the letter (e.g. d d d duck). • Repeat a few times using the **copy me method**. • Show the children the grapheme side of the card. Draw the letter formation over the grapheme as you say the sound. • Repeat a few times using the **copy me method**. The children can draw the letter formation over the grapheme as you say the sound together. • Play the **Grapheme game**. Show alternate sides of the card as the children call out. Repeat. • Play **Grapheme spotter** with the new GPC.	• Always say the sound when you say the mnemonic, including in the **copy me method** and **Grapheme game**. • Ensure there is lots of repetition of reading and saying the grapheme. • The children can draw the letter formation over the picture/grapheme as you say the sound together. • Play the **Grapheme game** several times to ensure the children have lots of practice. This will help move the grapheme into their long-term memory. • To play **Grapheme spotter**: 　• Add the new grapheme into a review pack of graphemes that the children already know. 　• Show the graphemes one by one. Ask the children to put their hands on their head and say the new sound each time they see the new way of writing the grapheme. • This should be very pacy.

Phases 2 and 3: Teaching a digraph/trigraph

You will need: Grapheme card for the Phase 2 or 3 GPC you are teaching.

What to do	Notes
Phoneme • Model the correct enunciation of the phoneme a few times. • Ensure the children can see how you make the sound. • Practise saying the sound together. Then ask the children to say it after you, several times.	• The Phase 2 digraphs (excluding double-letter digraphs) are 'ck', 'th', 'sh', 'ch', 'ng', 'nk' and 'qu'. • Ensure you use a clear voice. • Observe the children and check they are enunciating correctly. • You can find guidance for pronouncing the Phase 3 sounds on the Little Wandle website.

Grapheme
• Show the children the mnemonic/catchphrase side of the grapheme card, making a connection between the image, the sound and the catchphrase.
• Teach the catchphrase.
• Repeat a few times, using the **copy me method**.
• Use the digraph mantra *'two letters, one sound'*.
• Show the children the grapheme side of the card as you say the sound.
• Draw the letter formation over the grapheme as you say the sound.
• Repeat a few times, using the **copy me method**. The children can draw the letter formation over the picture as you say the sound together.
• Remind the children of the catchphrase.
• Play the **Grapheme game**. Show alternate sides of the card as the children call out. Repeat.
• Play **Grapheme spotter** with the new GPC.
	• Always say the sound when you say the catchphrase, including in the **copy me method** and **Grapheme game**.
	• The graphemes 'igh', 'ear' and 'air' are Phase 3 trigraphs – *'three letters, one sound'*.
	• Use a variety of 'voices' to say the catchphrase – high, low, loud, whisper, etc. The catchphrase is the 'hook' to help the children remember the grapheme – make sure it sticks!
	• To play **Grapheme spotter**:
	  • Add the new grapheme into a review pack of graphemes that the children already know.
	  • Show the graphemes one by one. Ask the children to put their hands on their head and say the new sound each time they see the new way of writing the grapheme.
	  • This should be very pacy.

Phase 5: Teaching a new GPC and oral blending

You will need: Grapheme card for the Phase 5 GPC you are teaching.

What to do	Notes
Teach: New phoneme • Introduce the new phoneme. • Model the correct enunciation a few times. Ensure the children can see how you make the sound. • Use the **copy me method** to get the children to practise saying the sound after you several times.	• Ensure you use a clear voice. • Observe the children and check they are all enunciating correctly. • You can find guidance for pronouncing the Phase 5 sounds on the Little Wandle website.
Teach: New grapheme • Show the children the previously taught graphemes for the new sound (in brackets on the planning grid). • **Say:** *Today, we are learning that (say sound) can look like this.* • Show the new grapheme card. • Ask the children to read the grapheme as you hide it and then show it several times. • If it is a digraph, use the mantra '*two letters, one sound*'. • Add the new grapheme card to the review pack. • Play **Grapheme spotter** with the new GPC.	• Take note of all previous linked graphemes in the weekly grid. There may be more than one. • To play **Grapheme spotter**: 　• Add the new grapheme into a review pack of graphemes that the children already know. 　• Show the graphemes one by one. Ask the children to put their hands on their head and say the new sound each time they see the new way of writing the grapheme. • This should be very pacy.
Teach: Oral blending • For each word: 　• Use the **copy me method**. 　• Sound-talk the word twice. 　• Ask the children to sound-talk the word and then blend to say the word. 　• Model sound-talking and blending the word. 　• Give a contextualising sentence or definition for the word, if needed.	• As the children sound-talk the word, nod your head to prompt them with the number of sounds.

Phases 2, 3 and 4: Oral blending

You will need: Phase 2 and 3 grapheme cards to make the words the children will read, images for **Match the words to the pictures** (from the website) for blending with pictures.

What to do	Notes
For each word: • Use the **copy me method**. • Sound-talk the word once. • Ask the children to sound-talk the word and then blend to say the word. • Model sound-talking and blending the word. • Give a contextualising sentence or definition for the word, if needed.	• As the children sound-talk the word, nod your head to prompt them with the number of sounds.
Blending with pictures • Tell the children that you are going to sound-talk the word for each picture and you want them to listen carefully and then point to the correct picture. • Put out four pictures so the children can easily point to them. • Sound-talk the word twice. • Ask the children to sound-talk the word and either blend aloud or in their head, and then point to the picture. • Model sound-talking and blending the word as you give feedback to the children.	• Oral blending is an important skill needed for reading, but it is not a prerequisite for learning to blend with graphemes or for learning to read graphemes. • Children who are not yet able to blend aloud can show their understanding by pointing to the pictures associated with the word. • You can use print-outs of the images provided for **Match the words to the pictures** for this activity.

Phase 2: Blending and reading words – super-supported method

You will need: Phase 2 grapheme cards to make the words the children will read.

What to do	Notes
• Use the grapheme cards and check which GPCs the children can read fluently. Use these GPCs to make up the words for this session. **Model reading the word** • Put out the grapheme cards. • Say the sounds. Pause as if you're thinking. Blend the word slowly, stretching the sounds out to help (e.g. mmmannn). • Say the sounds. Blend the word a bit faster. Then say the word. • Say the sounds. Blend the word at normal speed. Look like you're having a 'lightbulb' moment. Say the word. • Point to each grapheme as you say its phoneme. • Sweep and blend the word. **Together** • Ask the children to join in as you point to each grapheme as you say its phoneme, sweep and blend the word. **Children** • Ask the children to have a go at reading. • Ask them to say each phoneme as you point to each grapheme. • Ask them to blend as you sweep beneath the word. **Assess (one-to-one)** • If the child is successful, read another word with this method and then try the supported method (see page 37). • If the child is not successful, ask them to read the word with you. Then repeat the whole process for a few other words.	• Choose the method where the children will be successful – move to a less-supported method during the session. Aim for independent blending with word cards. • Make words with the GPCs that the children can read with ease. Do not make words with any GPCs that are not secure. • Always show the grapheme side to make the words. • Make sure the graphemes and words are directly in front of the children. • The children may well find it hard to blend the word successfully, even if they can read the sounds with ease. They will need daily practice and support to learn to blend – don't give up.

Phase 2: Blending and reading words – supported method

You will need: Phase 2 grapheme cards to make the words the children will read.

What to do	Notes

- Use the grapheme cards and check which GPCs the children can read fluently. Use these GPCs to make up the words for this session.
- For each word:
  - Put out the cards to make the word.
  - Model reading. Read and point to each grapheme. Sweep and blend.
 	
Children
- Ask the children to have a go at reading.
- Ask them to say each phoneme as you point to each grapheme.
- Ask them to blend as you sweep beneath the word.
 	
Together
- Ask the children to join in as you point to each grapheme as you say its phoneme, sweep and blend the word.
 	
Assess (one-to-one)
- If the child is successful, read another word with the supported method and then try the whisper method (see page 38).
- If the child is not successful, ask them to read the word with you. Then repeat the whole process for a few other words or go back to the super-supported method (see page 36).
 	
Assess: Mix it up (one-to-one outside the Rapid Catch-up lesson)
Choose two words you have already read. For each word:
- Mix up the cards. Put them into the correct order to make the word.
- Model reading. Read and point to each grapheme. Sweep and blend.
- Mix up the cards and give them to the children.
- Ask the children to put the cards into the correct order to make the word.
- Ask them to point to each grapheme and say each phoneme.
- Ask them to sweep beneath the word and blend to read the word.
	- Make words with the GPCs that the children can read with ease. Do not make words with any GPCs that are not secure.
	- Always show the grapheme side to make the words.
	- Make sure the graphemes and words are directly in front of the children.
	- The children may well find it hard to blend the word successfully, even if they can read the sounds with ease. They will need daily practice and support to learn to blend – don't give up.
	- You may want to model fewer words each session as the children become more confident and move to the next stage of blending more quickly.
	- The children can take over the pointing and sweeping when they are reading the word as soon as they are confident and want to!

Phase 2: Blending and reading words – whisper method

You will need: Phase 2 grapheme cards to make the words the children will read.

What to do	Notes

- Use the grapheme cards and check which GPCs the children can read fluently. Use these GPCs to make up the words for this session.
- For each word:
  - Put out the cards to make the word.
  - Whisper and point to each grapheme. Sweep and blend.
 	
Children
- Ask the children to have a go at reading.
- Ask them to say each phoneme as you point to each grapheme.
- Ask them to blend as you sweep beneath the word.
 	
Together
- Ask the children to join in as you point to each grapheme as you say its phoneme, sweep and blend the word.
 	
Assess (one-to-one)
- If the child is successful, read another word with this method, this time without whisper blending, and then try independent reading (see page 39) with word cards.
- If the child is not successful, ask them to read the word with you. Then repeat the whole process for a few other words.
 	
Assess: Mix it up (one-to-one outside the Rapid Catch-up lesson)
- Choose two words you have already read. For each word:
  - Mix up the cards. Put them into the correct order to make the word.
  - Model reading. Read and point to each grapheme. Sweep and blend.
  - Mix up the cards and give them to the children.
  - Ask the children to put the cards into the correct order to make the word.
  - Ask them to point to each grapheme and say each phoneme.
  - Ask them to sweep beneath the word and blend to read the word.
	- Make words with the GPCs that the children can read with ease. Do not make words with any GPCs that are not secure.
	- Always show the grapheme side to make the words.
	- Make sure the graphemes and words are directly in front of the children.
	- You may want to model fewer words each session as the children become more confident and move to the next stage of blending more quickly.
	- The children can take over the pointing and sweeping when they are reading the word as soon as they are confident and want to!
	- This is the bridge to independent reading. Make sure the children have a go at reading a word without any support – with the grapheme cards – in every session.
	- Make sure the class teacher and parent/carer are told which GPCs the children are making words with, so they can practise them with the children at other times.

Phase 2: Blending and reading words – independent reading

You will need: Phase 2 word cards, Phase 2 grapheme cards for a quick review.

What to do	Notes

• Start the session with a quick review of Phase 2 GPCs using the grapheme cards.
• For each word:
  • Put the word card (sound-button side out) in front of the children.
  • If applicable, ask if they can see any digraphs in the word.
 	
Children
• Ask the children to sound-talk each grapheme and then blend to read the word aloud.
• Ask them to point to each grapheme and then sweep beneath as they blend. Do NOT help them.
 	
Together
• Ask the children to join in as they point to each grapheme and say its phoneme, sweep and blend the word.
 	
Assess (one-to-one)
• If the child is successful, read another word with this method, using the word cards.
• If the child is confident, challenge them to read without overt blending. Model blending in your head to read the word aloud then ask them to have a go themselves.
• If the child is not successful, ask them to read the word with you and then go back to the whisper method (see page 38) to support them.
	• Only use words with the GPCs that the children can read with ease. Do not make words with any GPCs that are not secure.
	• Start with words that don't have digraphs.
	• When the children are confident reading these words, start to use words with the Phase 2 digraphs 'ck', 'll', 'ff', 'ss', 'zz', 'qu', 'sh', 'ch', 'th', 'ng' and 'nk'.
	• If the children are confident, challenge them to read without overt blending – blending in their heads to read the word aloud.
	• Make sure the class teacher and parent/carer are told which GPCs the children are making words with, so they can practise them with the children at other times.

Phases 3 and 5: Reading words

You will need: Phase 3/5 grapheme cards for a quick review, Phase 3/5 word cards.

What to do	Notes

• Start the session with a quick review of Phase 3/5 GPCs using the grapheme cards.
• For each word:
  • Put the word card (sound-button side out) in front of the children.
  • Ask if they can see any digraphs in the word.
 	
Children
• Ask the children to sound-talk each grapheme and then blend to read the word aloud.
• Ask them to point to each grapheme and then sweep beneath as they blend. Do NOT help them.
 	
Together
• Ask the children to join in as they point to each grapheme and say its phoneme, sweep and blend the word.
 	
Assess (one-to-one)
• If the child is successful, read another word with this method.
• If the child is confident, challenge them to read without overt blending – blending in their head to read the word aloud.
• If the child is not successful, ask them to read the word with you and then go back to the whisper method (see page 38) to support them.
	• Only use words with the GPCs that the children can read with ease. Do not make words with any GPCs that are not secure.
	• Choose four to six words to read in the session.
	• Make sure the class teacher and parent/carer are told which words the children are reading in these sessions, so they can practise them with the children at other times.

Win it! (one-to-one) • Use the side of the word card without sound buttons for this activity. • Add one of the new word cards to the review pack. Make sure it is close to the top of the pack. • Each time the child reads the new word, stop the game, shuffle the cards and move the card back a bit in the pack. • Shuffle and repeat, incrementally moving the new card back. • Each time the child reads the new word correctly, they 'win' the card. • You can add another word to the pack if there is time.	• Have a pack of four to six words the children can read with confidence as the review pack for **Win it!**

All phases: Reading words ending with –s and –es

You will need: Word cards ending in –s and –es, grapheme cards to make the words (optional).

What to do	Notes
Oral blending words ending with 's' /s/ • Blend the word without the 's'. • Then go through the same process with the 's' at the end. **Reading words ending with 's' /s/** • Hide the 's' on the word card and ask the children to read the word. • Reveal the 's' and ask the children to read the whole word. **Orally blending words ending with 's' and 'es' when 's' and 'es' makes the /z/ sound** • Blend the word without the 's' or 'es'. • Then go through the same process with the 's' or 'es' at the end. • Help the children to hear the /z/ sound that the 's' or 'es' makes. **Reading words ending with 's' and 'es' /z/** • Hide the 's' or 'es' on the word card and ask the children to read the word. • Then reveal the 's' or 'es' and ask the children to read the whole word. • Remind the children of the /z/ sound that the 's' or 'es' makes.	• This activity can be slowed down by using the grapheme cards to make the words. • Make the words without the suffix '–s' or '–es' and ask the children to read the words. • Add the 's' or 'e' and 's' grapheme cards to make the words. • The suffix '–s' and '–es' at the end of words can create plurals and the present tense of verbs.

All phases: Reading tricky words

You will need: Tricky word to learn and tricky words for **Win it!**

What to do	Notes
- Show the tricky word on a card. - Read the decodable parts of the word. Point to the 'tricky bit'* and tell the children the sound that this grapheme makes. - Model reading the word. - Ask the children to read the word a few times independently.	- Make sure the class teacher and parent/carer are told which words the children are reading in these sessions, so they can practise them with the children at other times.
Win it! (one-to-one) - Add the new tricky word card to the review pack. Make sure it is close to the top of the pack. - Each time the child reads the new tricky word, stop the game, shuffle the cards and move the card back a bit in the pack. - Shuffle and repeat, incrementally moving the new tricky word card back. - Each time the child reads the new word correctly, they 'win' the card.	- Have a pack of four to six tricky words that the children can read with confidence as the review pack for **Win it!**

*Use the additional 'Support for tricky words' guidance on the website to help identify the tricky bit in each word.

All phases: Reading longer words

You will need: Phase 3, 4 or 5 word cards of words with more than one syllable.

What to do	Notes
Model chunking the first word (e.g. ladder) • Cover the second part of the word (so the card shows 'ladd'). • Sound-talk the first part of the word using the point and sweep actions: l-a-dd lad • Reveal the second part of the word (-er) and repeat the step above. • Blend as you sweep under the whole word: ladder **Children** • Put the card in front of the children and cover the second part of the word. • Ask the children to sound-talk each grapheme and then blend the first part of the word aloud. • Reveal the second part of the word and repeat the step above. • Ask the children to point to each grapheme and then sweep beneath as they blend the whole word. Do NOT help them. **Together** • Ask the children to join in to read the word all the way through. Point to each grapheme and sweep beneath the word as you read. **For each subsequent word** • Put the word card in front of the children. • Ask the children to identify the trigraphs/digraphs. • Cover the second part of the word. • Ask the children to sound-talk each grapheme and then blend the first part of the word aloud. • Reveal the second part of the word and repeat the step above. • Ask the children to point to each grapheme and then sweep beneath as they blend the whole word. Do NOT help them.	• Choose four or five words to read in a session. • Model the procedure for the first word, to ensure the children know what to do. • Always cover up the syllables for the children as they won't be able to work these out for themselves. • Make sure the class teacher and parent/carer are told which words the children are reading in these sessions, so they can practise them with the children at other times.
Win it! (one-to-one lessons only) • Use the side of the word card without sound buttons for this activity. • Add one of the new longer word cards to the review pack. Make sure it is close to the top of the pack. • Each time the child reads the new word, stop the game, shuffle the cards and move the card back a bit in the pack. • Shuffle and repeat, incrementally moving the new card back. • Each time the child reads the new word correctly, they 'win' the card. • You can add another word to the pack if there is time.	• Include some single-syllable words in the **Win it!** activity.

All phases: Reading words with speedy digraph recognition

You will need: Phase 2, 3 and 5 grapheme cards for a quick review; Phase 2, 3, 4 and 5 word cards.

What to do	Notes

• Start the session with a quick review of GPCs using the Phase 2 and 3 or Phase 5 grapheme cards.
• For each word:
  • Put the word card (show side without sound buttons) in front of the children.
  • Ask if they can see any digraphs in the word. If they cannot, show them the appropriate grapheme card, remind them what it says, and point to the matching grapheme in the word.
 	
Children
• Ask the children to sound-talk each grapheme and then blend to read the word aloud.
• Ask them to point to each grapheme and then sweep beneath as they blend. Do NOT help them.
 	
Together
• Ask the children to join in as they point to each grapheme and say its phoneme, sweep and blend the word.
 	
Assess
• If the children are successful, read another word with this method.
• If they continue to find it difficult to identify the digraphs/trigraphs, model the process using the whisper method (see page 38).
	• Only use words with Phase 2, 3 or 5 digraphs/trigraphs that the children can read with ease.
	• Use words with one digraph only to start with (e.g. seed, green). Build up to words with more than one digraph (e.g. sheep) once these words are secure.
	• Choose four to six words to read in the session.
	• Put aside any GPCs that the children cannot read automatically. Ensure these GPCs are taught in the next session using 'Phases 2 and 3: Teaching digraph/trigraph' (page 33), 'Phase 5: Teaching a new GPC and oral blending' (page 34) and/or 'All phases: Precision teaching' (page 53).
	• Do not stop teaching these GPCs until they are all automatic.
	• Make sure the class teacher and parent/carer are told which words the children are reading in these sessions, so they can practise them with the children at other times.

Win it! (one-to-one lessons only) • Use the side of the word card without sound buttons for this activity. • Add one of the new word cards to the review pack. Make sure it is close to the top of the pack. • Each time the child reads the new word, stop the game, shuffle the cards and move the card back a bit in the pack. • Shuffle and repeat, incrementally moving the new card back. • Each time the child reads the new word correctly, they 'win' the card. • You can add another word to the pack if there is time.	• Have a pack of four to six words the children can read with confidence as the review pack for **Win it!**.

All phases: Reading words with/without overt blending

You will need: Word cards that the children can read but with continued use of overt blending.

What to do	Notes

Reading with overt blending
• For each word:
  • Put the word card in front of the children.
  • Ask if they can see any digraphs in the word.
 	
Children
• Ask the children to sound-talk each grapheme and then blend to read the word aloud.
• Ask them to point to each grapheme and then sweep beneath as they blend. Do NOT help them.
 	
Together
• Ask the children to join in to read the word by blending 'in their heads'. Sweep beneath the word as you read.
 	
Assess (one-to-one)
• If the child is successful, read another word with this method.
• If the child is confident, move on to reading without overt blending – blending 'in their head' to read the word aloud.
 	
Reading without overt blending
For each word:
• Put the word card in front of the children.
• Ask them to point to any digraphs in the word and say what they are.
• Tell the children to read the words on the cards without sounding out.
• Ask them to sweep beneath the word as they read.
• Repeat.
 	
Assess
• If the child is successful, read another word with this method.
• If the child is still blending aloud, go back to **Reading with overt blending** above.
	• Use the word cards without the sound buttons.
	• Make sure the class teacher and parent/carer are told which words the children are reading in these sessions, so that they can practise them with the children at other times.

Phase 4: Reading words with adjacent consonants

You will need: Phase 2 and 3 grapheme cards to make the words the children will read, Phase 4 word cards if the children progress to independent reading.

What to do	Notes

- Use the grapheme cards and check which GPCs the children can read fluently. Use these GPCs to make up the words for this session.
- For each word:
  - Put out the cards to make the word.
  - Model reading. Whisper and point to each grapheme. Sweep and blend.
 	
Children
- Ask the children to have a go at reading.
- Ask them to say each phoneme as you point to each grapheme.
- Ask them to blend as you sweep beneath the word.
 	
Together
- Ask the children to join in as you point to each grapheme as you say its phoneme, sweep and blend the word.
 	
Assess
- If the child is successful, read another word with this method, this time without whisper blending, and then try independent reading (see page 39) with word cards.
- If the child is not successful, ask them to read the word with you. Then repeat the whole process for a few other words.
 	
Assess: Mix it up (outside the Rapid Catch-up lesson)
- Choose two words you have already read.
- For each word:
  - Mix up the cards. Put them into the correct order to make the word.
  - Model reading. Read and point to each grapheme. Sweep and blend.
  - Mix up the cards and give them to the children.
  - Ask the children to put the cards into the correct order to make the word.
  - Ask them to point to each grapheme and say each phoneme.
  - Ask them to sweep beneath the word and blend to read the word.
	- Start by making words with adjacent consonants and short vowel sounds.
	- Words with two adjacent consonants at the end (e.g. went, help) are easier to start with.
	- Move to two adjacent consonants at the beginning of words (e.g. drum, smell), before reading words with three adjacent consonants (e.g. strap, strong)
	- You can find a full list of Phase 4 words on page 65.
	- If needed, repeat the process with adjacent consonants and long vowel sounds.
	- Make sure the class teacher and parent/carer are told which words the children are reading in these sessions, so they can practise them with the children at other times.

Phase 5: Reading words with graphemes that have more than one sound e.g. 'ow' /ow/ /oa/

You will need: Phase 2 and 3 grapheme cards (picture side), images to match Phase 5 alternative sounds (available on the Little Wandle website), Phase 3, 4 and 5 word cards that include the grapheme you are teaching.

What to do	Notes

• Explain that the grapheme makes more than one sound.
• Display the picture side of the Phase 2 or 3 grapheme card and an image that matches the other sound the grapheme makes.
• Point to each card. Say the two sounds in context, to help the children really 'hear' the two different phonemes e.g. /ow/ 'wow owl' and /oa/ 'snow'.
• Tell the children to say the correct sound as you point to the images.
 	
Sort the words by phoneme
• Tell the children they will now read words and work out which image they should go under, according to the sound the grapheme makes.
• For each word:
  • Put the word card in front of the children.
  • Ask them to identify the grapheme.
  • Read each word.
  • Ask them to help you sort the word to the appropriate sound.
 	
Assess (one-to-one)
• If the child is successful, read and sort another word.
• If the child reads the word with the incorrect pronunciation for the grapheme, model the correct pronunciation for the grapheme and return the word to the pack of words for the child to try later.
	• This activity is useful for children who can identify the graphemes but find attributing the correct phoneme difficult.
	• If any children cannot identify the digraphs with ease, then they need: **Reading words with speedy digraph recognition** (page 44).
	• Please see the list of **Graphemes with more than one sound** on page 69.
	• Use six to eight words for this activity. Use word cards without sound buttons.
	• Some words have more than one pronunciation, e.g. 'read', 'wind'. Discuss these with the children and use them in contextualising sentences.
	• Make sure the class teacher and parent/carer are told which words the children are reading in these sessions, so that they can practise them with the children at other times.

Phase 5: Reading words containing a split vowel digraph

You will need: Word cards for Phase 5 split vowel digraph words.

What to do	Notes

- Model how to read the first word (e.g. home).
- Show the word card (sound buttons showing).
- Read each sound as you point. Point to the arch as you read the split vowel digraph.
- Sweep beneath as you blend the whole word.
- Tell the children that the arch shows that the two letters are making one sound, even though they are not next to each other.
 	
Children
- Ask the children to sound-talk each grapheme and then blend to read the word aloud.
- Ask them to point to each grapheme and then sweep beneath as they blend. Do NOT help them.
- For each subsequent word:
  - Put the word card in front of the children.
  - Ask if they can see any digraphs/split vowel digraphs in the word.
  - Ask them to point to each grapheme and then sweep beneath as they blend. Do NOT help them.
 	
Together
- Ask the children to join in to read the word by blending 'in their heads'. Sweep beneath the word as you read.
- Aim to read the words without overt blending as described below.
- For each word:
  - Put the word card in front of the children.
  - Ask them to point to any digraphs/split vowel digraphs in the word and say what they are.
  - Tell the children to read the words on the cards without sounding out.
  - Ask them to sweep beneath the word as they read.
  - Repeat.
	- Use the word cards with the sound buttons.
	- Over time move to showing the words without the sound buttons, so the children become expert at spotting the split vowel digraph.
	- Ensure lots of repetition so the children become confident in reading these types of words.
	- Aim for the children to read the words without overt blending, so they are growing their fluency and accuracy.

Prompt cards: Practise and apply

Phase 5: Grow the code

You will need: Phase 2, 3 and 5 grapheme cards, word cards for **Best bets***.

What to do	Notes
Grow the code • Ask the children to write down as many different spellings of that day's 'Grow the code' phoneme as they know. • Take feedback. • Show the children the 'Grow the code' graphemes – did they get them all?	• Pointing out the 'Grow the code' graphemes should be pacy. • Refer to the 'Grow the code' chart to explore all the possible GPCs.
Best bets • Display all the 'Grow the code' graphemes for the lesson. • Ask the children to talk to their partner and say all the phonemes they know for each grapheme. Take feedback. • Tell the children they are going to sort the words by grapheme. • Ask the children to read the words. • Work together to sort each word under the appropriate grapheme. • Discuss which graphemes are most common and where they are located in words. Are there any patterns?	• Use the word-only side of the cards – the children have already read these words. • Use minimal language for instructions to ensure the children can focus on the reading of the word. • Discuss how the words are formed and where the GPCs are within the words. Link these spelling patterns to other similar words and help the children make connections between the words and their likely spellings.

*You will find list of words suitable for **Best bets** in the Rapid Catch-up area of the Little Wandle website.

All phases: Change it

You will need: Grapheme cards for the phase you are working on.

What to do	Notes

Change it!
• For each word:
  • Put out the cards to make the word.
  • Ask the children to sound-talk each grapheme and then blend to read the word aloud.
  • Point to each grapheme and then sweep beneath the word to signal blending. Do NOT help the children.
  • Look at the children (not at the cards).
  • Read the word together.
• **Say:** *Change it!* Take one grapheme away and replace it with the new grapheme to change the word.
• Ask the children to read the new grapheme. Remind them of what the word said before. **Say:** *Now let's read a new word.*
• Repeat the procedure above.
	• You will need the grapheme cards to make all the words listed in the weekly grid.
	• Follow the order of the words listed in the weekly grid, so that the words change by one grapheme at a time.
	• Use this time to help the children practise blending with less support from you – but if they struggle at all, go back to the teacher-led blending method to ensure all the children are blending successfully.
	• This activity helps the children to see how the graphemes within the word affect how the word sounds. It should help the children to identify individual sounds in all parts of the word.
	• This activity will aid reading and spelling skills.

All phases: Match the words to the pictures

You will need: **Match the words to the pictures** resource for the phase that you are working on.

What to do	Notes

• Display the numbered pictures and then hide them.
• Hold up each word and ask the children to:
  • identify the digraphs/trigraphs
  • read the word (after they have read the word reveal the pictures again)
  • show which picture matches the word by holding up the appropriate number of fingers.
• Read the word again without any overt blending.
	• Ensure the children know what all the pictures represent. This is especially important for children who are new to speaking English or have English as an additional language.

All phases: Mix it up (spelling with grapheme cards – one-to-one)

You will need: Grapheme cards for the phase that you are working on.

What to do	Notes

• Display the grapheme cards you need to spell the word, as well as some extra grapheme cards as distractors.
 	
Oral practice
• Use the **copy me method** to say the word and then segment it.
• Count the sounds in the word.
 	
Spelling with grapheme cards
• Model spelling the word with grapheme cards:
  • Segment the word and choose the correct grapheme for the first sound.
  • Place the card on the table.
  • Continue with all the sounds until you have spelled the word.
  • Read the word.
• Mix up the cards and ask the child to spell the word independently by segmenting and choosing the correct graphemes.
• Ask the child to read the word.
	• This activity works best in a one-to-one session but you could try it with pairs or a small group if you have enough grapheme cards.
	• Use segmenting fingers to support the child to segment sounds.
	• If there is a digraph/trigraph, use the mantra *'two/three letters, one sound'*.

All phases: Spelling (without grapheme cards)

You will need: Mini whiteboards and pens.

What to do	Notes
• Use the **copy me method** to say the word and then segment it. • Count the sounds in the word. • Model spelling the word. • Ask the children to say each sound before you write it down. If there is a digraph/trigraph, use the mantra *'two/three letters, one sound'* to remind the children. Say the letter name after you write it. • Hide the word. • Ask the children to spell the word. Tell them to segment as they write. • Show your spelling and check together. • Repeat for the other words.	• Use segmenting fingers to support the children to segment sounds. • Minimise your language but remind the children to segment as they write. • Observe and support the children as they write. Ensure they use correct letter formation but do not let this detract from the lesson. (Handwriting must be taught as a separate lesson.)

All phases: Spelling tricky words

You will need: Mini whiteboards and pens.

What to do	Notes
• Use the **copy me method** to say the word and then segment it. • Count the sounds in the word. • Model spelling the word. Tell the children which part of the word is tricky. • Ask the children to say each sound before you write it down. Remind them how you spell the 'tricky bit'. • Hide the word. • Ask the children to spell the word. • Show your spelling and check together.	• Observe and support the children as they write. If they need scaffolds, remind them how to write the 'tricky bit' of the word.

Phase 5: Sort the words by grapheme/phoneme

You will need: The word cards identified on the weekly grid, images to sort the words under (from the website).

What to do	Notes

Sort the words by grapheme
• Display a suitable image for each grapheme.
• Ask the children to say the grapheme and word for each image e.g. 'ear' 'bear' and 'are' 'square'.
• Identify the common phoneme e.g. /air/.
• Hold up each word and ask the children to:
  • identify any digraphs/trigraphs
  • read each word
  • help you sort the word to the appropriate grapheme/image
  • read the word again.
 	
Sort the words by phoneme
• Display a suitable image for each phoneme.
• Ask the children to read the words for each image e.g. 'sky' and 'baby'.
• Identify the common grapheme e.g. 'y'.
• Hold up each word and ask the children to:
  • identify any digraphs/trigraphs
  • read the word.
• Model reading the words with both pronunciations.
• Ask the children to sort the word to the appropriate phoneme under the correct catchphrase.
• Read the word again.
	• Use the word-only side of the word cards – the children have already read these words in previous lessons.
	• Use minimal language for instructions, to ensure the children can focus on the reading of the word.
	• Pointing out the digraphs/trigraphs should be pacy.
	• Watch the children carefully to ensure that they are all blending.

Phases 4 and 5: Read the sentence

You will need: A copy of the sentence for the children to read (see weekly grids), written in advance of the lesson on a flipchart or large sheet of paper (or from the website).

What to do	Notes

• Display the phrase or sentence.
• Ask the children to identify any digraphs they can see. Take feedback.
• Point to the words with digraphs.
• Ask the children to read one or two of the words. Do NOT read the words to the children.
 	
Tricky words
• Ask the children to identify any tricky words they can see.
• Point to the tricky words and ask the children to read them together.
 	
Children read
• Ask the children to read aloud as you point to the words. Remind them to sound out any words they are not sure of.
 	
Second read
• Ask the children to read again. Pause and ask individual children to read key words (i.e. words including a new grapheme) in the sentence.
 	
Read together
• Read the phrase or sentence together.
• Point to each word. Read at a steady pace.
	• When asking the children to read the words:
	  • Sweep underneath the word so that all the children can then read it together.
	  • As you read together, sweep underneath longer words.
	• Draw the children's attention to the capital letters and full stops in sentences.

Phases 4 and 5: Write the sentence

You will need: Mini whiteboards and pens.

What to do	Notes

Prepare
• Say the sentence.
• Use the **copy me method** to practise saying the sentence until the children are confident.
• Write the sentence. Model how you:
  • use capital letters and punctuation
  • segment to spell
  • remember digraphs/trigraphs
  • remember the 'tricky bit' of tricky words.
• Hide the sentence.
	• Say the sentence multiple times until the children can say it to a partner easily.

Write • Ask the children to write the sentence. • Check the sentence together. • Ask the children to check and correct their spelling.	• Give the children time to check errors and correct them. • If there is a common error/misconception, model making it and correcting it. Explain where the mistake is and how to correct it.

Prompt card: Review lesson

All phases: Precision teaching (graphemes/words/tricky words)
- Use this activity to give the children repeated practice, which will help them gain fluency and aid automatic recall of GPCs.
- You can also use this precision teaching method with words and tricky words – just set up the grid with the appropriate words that need additional practice.

You will need: The grapheme card for the GPC you are teaching, a copy of the **Precision teaching grids** (see page 70).

In advance of the lesson:
- Write the focus grapheme at least twice in each row, in random places.
- Write three other graphemes that the children know fluently into the other spaces on the grid.

What to do	Notes
Focus grapheme • Show the children the grapheme side of the grapheme card. Draw the letter formation over the grapheme as you say the sound. • Repeat a few times, using the **copy me method**. • The children can draw the letter formation over the grapheme as you say the sound together. **Grid** • Put the filled-in grapheme grid in front of the children. • Model pointing to the focus grapheme on the grid and reading it aloud. • Point to the focus grapheme on the grid and ask the children to read. • Ask the children to find the focus grapheme, point to it and read. • Now ask the children to read all the graphemes in each line as you point. • If the children do not recognise a grapheme, tell them the sound, get them to repeat and continue. • Repeat, building on fluency.	• You can also use the Phase 2 and 3 grapheme mat, or the Phase 2, 3 and 5 'Grow the code' mat to point to graphemes that the children need to practise to gain fluency. • Choose up to four graphemes to practise and point to them in random order on the mat. • This method can be used with words as well as GPCs.

Note: Prompt cards for other teaching methods and activities used in the Review lesson can be found in the 'Teach and practise' section (pages 32 to 48). Prompt cards for the reading practice sessions are on pages 54 to 61.

Prompt cards: Reading practice sessions

Phases 2, 3 and 4: Reading blending practice books

You will need: Blending practice book, grapheme cards for the GPCs covered in the book (Phases 2 and 3 only).

Note that the three reads detailed in the 'Practise and apply' section below should be done in three different sessions. Do the 'Pre-read' activities before each of the three reads.

Pre-read

What to do	Notes
Quick review: GPCs • Ask the children to read speedy sounds. • Use all cards – **grapheme side only**. (Only show the mnemonic side if the children are unsure). • Shuffle. Repeat. **Grapheme chart in the blending practice book (Phases 2 and 3)** Ask the children to read as you point to the graphemes in any order. **Tricky words** • Remind the children of how to read any tricky words in the tricky word box. Point to the parts of the word that are decodable and identify the 'tricky bit'. • Read the word together. • Ask the children to read the word. **Connect** • Discuss the front cover, blurb and title of the book.	• Ensure you practise the graphemes before reading the book. • For Phase 4, you will see that there are words to practise reading words ending in –s and –es (see page 41) and longer words (see page 43). Ask the children to sound-talk each word and blend. Model the chunking process where needed.

Practise and apply

What to do	Notes
Read 1: Decoding • Ask the children to sound-talk each word and blend. • Ask them to find the image that matches the word/phrase in the picture. • When they have found the image matching the word/phrase, ask them to verify their answer by turning the page to see the matching image. • Ask them to read the word/phrase again. **After reading** • Revise any specific difficulties. • Read the whole book, demonstrating fluency and prosody, asking the children to follow. • Use your assessments from the reading session to address any common errors with GPCs, specific words in the book or tricky words. • Use the activity on pages 14 to 15 of the blending practice book to develop comprehension and language.	• Check that the only strategy used to read the words is decoding. • Do not intervene too quickly. Encourage children having difficulty to try to sound out a word for themselves before supporting. • If children are struggling to recall the grapheme or word, point to the grapheme card to prompt them. • If children are struggling to read a word, use grapheme cards to make the word and model reading it using the appropriate teacher-led blending method. • After reading, quickly reteach any GPCs, words or tricky words that the children struggled with. • Review these within a pack of other GPCs, words or tricky words that are secure. • Use your assessments from the reading session to identify any words that need teaching. Use grapheme cards to make the word and model reading it using the appropriate teacher-led blending method.

What to do	Notes
Read 2: Vocabulary • Ask the children to sound-talk each word and blend. • Ask them to find the image that matches the word/phrase in the picture. • When they have found the image matching the word/phrase, ask them to turn over and try to read the word/phrase without overt blending. **After reading** • Go back over the three full pages and discuss the images. Encourage the children to talk about details that stand out for them. • Use a dialogic talk model to expand on their ideas and recast them in full sentences as naturally as possible. • Work together to expand vocabulary by naming objects in the illustrations that the children do not know. • Use your assessments from the reading session to address any common errors with GPCs or words.	• Initially, the children may sound out the graphemes in each word. Encourage them to blend and say the word. Then encourage them to sound it out in their heads.
Read 3: Comprehension • Ask the children to read each word without overt blending. • Ask them to find the image that matches the word/phrase in the picture. • When they have found the image matching the word/phrase, ask them to turn over and try to read the word/phrase as fluently as possible. **After reading** • Make connections between the illustrations and the child's experiences in school/at home. • Use a dialogic talk model to expand on their ideas and recast them in full sentences as naturally as possible. • Use the comprehension notes in the back of the book to support teaching comprehension.	• Encourage the children to sound out the words in their head. • Always ensure the children use decoding strategies to read words, rather than guessing.

All phases: Reading the 7+ books – decoding

You will need: Grapheme cards for the GPCs covered in the book.

In advance of the lesson: Download the focus words, tricky words, vocabulary and comprehension guidance from collins.co.uk/BigCatLittleWandleL&SRevised.

Pre-read

What to do	Notes

Recall of GPCs that will appear in the book
• **Say:** *Let's read the sounds that we will read in the book.*
• Show each grapheme card at a consistent pace to ensure quick recognition of sounds.
• Pick up any misconceptions, model the correct pronunciation and practise again.
• If the children cannot fluently read one or two graphemes, reteach, reverting to the mnemonics or catchphrase, if necessary, then practise.
• Repeat for tricky words that appear in the book.
	• Ensure good flashcard control:
	  • Take care to turn the cards at a fairly rapid pace.
	  • Hold the cards at the edge.
	  • Ensure the cards are at a height that is easy for the children to see.
	• Pay close attention to children at risk of falling behind, to ensure good participation.
	• Look at the children (not at the cards) to assess their reading.
	• Do not read or mouth the sounds to the children.
	• If the children cannot read most of these graphemes fluently, this book is unlikely to be matched to their secure phonic knowledge and is not appropriate.
	• If the children can't read a tricky word, identify the 'tricky bit' by pointing to the grapheme and saying its sound.

Read words • **Say:** *We are going to read some of the words from the book fluently. Let's check we know what to do.* • Hold up a word and ask the children to look for any digraphs. Then ask the children to sound out the word and blend out loud. • **Say:** *Let's read this fluently. Remember, that means blending in your heads, without sounding out.* • **Say:** *Show each word and sweep beneath the word to signal blending.*	• Watch the children carefully to ensure all children are blending in their heads. • If the children have difficulty, revert to sounding out and blending. • If the word has one or more digraphs, ask them to identify these first. Use the mantra *'two letters, one sound'* to reinforce the learning. • You may want to use images of the new vocabulary to secure understanding.
New vocabulary • Show the children any new vocabulary on word cards and practise reading them, sounding out, if necessary. • Ask if they know what the word means. • If they do not know, teach the meaning. • Put the new word in context. • Ask the children to say the word.	• Before the children start reading the book, place the grapheme cards on the table for the children to refer to if they get stuck when reading.

Practise and apply

What to do	Notes
• Ask the children to read independently. • Ask them to read the words without sounding out each word aloud, but remind them they can sound out and blend words if they need to. • If you are working with a group, tap in to listen to each child read, and check that they are reading every word. **If there is time:** • Practise reading longer or more challenging words in the book. • Revise any specific difficulties with individual children. • Read the whole book, demonstrating fluency and prosody, asking the children to follow.	• Check that the only strategy used to read the words is decoding. • Do not intervene too quickly. Encourage a child having difficulty to try to sound out a word for themselves before supporting. If a child is struggling to recall the grapheme or word, point to the grapheme card to prompt them. • Initially, the children may sound out the graphemes. Encourage them to blend and say the word. Then encourage them to sound it out in their heads. • Remember that if the children cannot read most of the words fluently, the book is unlikely to be matched to their secure phonic knowledge and is not appropriate.

Review

What to do	Notes
• Use your assessments from the reading session to address any errors with GPCs, specific words in the book or tricky words. • Use the teaching notes in the back of the book for further support with decoding practice.	• Remember the focus of this session is decoding. • Quickly reteach any GPCs, words or tricky words that the children struggled with. • Review these within a pack of other GPCs, words or tricky words that are secure.

All phases: Reading the 7+ books – prosody

You will need: Grapheme cards for the GPCs covered in the book.

In advance of the lesson: Download the focus words, tricky words, vocabulary and comprehension guidance from collins.co.uk/BigCatLittleWandleL&SRevised.

Pre-read

What to do	Notes
Quick review of GPCs • **Say:** *Let's read the sounds that we will read in the book.* • Show each grapheme card and ask the children to say the sounds out loud. • Pick up any misconceptions, model the correct pronunciation and practise again. • If any children cannot fluently read some of the graphemes, reteach, reverting to the mnemonics or catchphrase, if necessary, then practise. **Quick review of tricky words** • Ask the children to read the words on the cards without sounding out. • Remind them that this means blending in their heads. • Show each card and sweep beneath the word to signal blending. **Vocabulary** • Check the children have remembered the meaning of the new vocabulary practised in the decoding session.	• The children will have covered this before in the decoding session. If they are confident, keep this part of the session short and quick. • Focus on any sounds and words that the children were uncertain of in the previous session. • Add any other sounds and words that caused difficulty. • Remember that repetition is valuable, even when the children seem to know the sounds and words already. Repetition secures the knowledge in the long-term memory. • Pay close attention to any children at risk of falling behind, to ensure good participation. • Before the children start reading the book, place the grapheme cards on the table for the children to refer to if they get stuck when reading.

Practise and apply

What to do	Notes

Read the book
• The reading should be quicker this time.
• Ask the children to read independently.
• Ask them to read the words without sounding out each word aloud, but remind them they can sound out and blend words if they need to.
• If you are working with more than one child, tap in to listen to each child read, and check that they are reading every word.
 	
Read with prosody
• Ask the children to turn to the pre-selected pages. Tell them they are going to practise reading with prosody so they can read aloud with meaning.
• Think aloud. For each sentence, explain how you are going to read with prosody.
• Draw attention to the features of the sentence that tell you how to say it:
  • verbs used for speech, e.g. 'shouted'
  • punctuation, e.g. an exclamation mark to show feeling or ellipses to build suspense
  • characters' feelings.
• Model reading one sentence with prosody.
• Ask the children to read the sentence with you with prosody.
• **Say:** *Let's see if we can read it with even more expression.*
• Read it together again.
• Ask the children to try themselves.
• Repeat with other sentences.
 	
If there is time:
• Ask the children to carry on reading the rest of the book with prosody.
	• Check that the only strategy used to read the words is decoding.
	• Do not intervene too quickly. Encourage a child having difficulty to try to sound out the word for themselves before supporting. If a child is struggling to recall the grapheme or word, point to the grapheme card to prompt them.
	• Initially, the children may sound out the graphemes. Encourage them to blend and say the word. Then encourage them to sound it out in their heads.
	• Check that any children who had difficulty with particular graphemes in the pre-read session are reading them correctly.
	• Select two double-page spreads (two pages facing each other). Choose pages with interesting speech verbs and punctuation.
	• Tap in to hear the children reading with prosody.

Review

What to do	Notes
Spelling **GPCs** • Ask the children to write down one of the sounds from the book. • Write the spelling of the sound on the board. Check the spelling together. • Ask the children to check carefully to see if they spelled it correctly. If they didn't, ask them to write the grapheme again. • Repeat with another sound. **Words** • Select a word from the book with known GPCs. Say it, segment it and count the sounds, e.g. *may: m-ay – that's two sounds*. • Ask the children to segment the word and write it. • Write the spelling on the board. Check the spelling together. Ask the children to check their spelling carefully and fix any errors. • Repeat with another word that has just one different GPC, e.g. 'pay'. **If there is time:** • Practise spelling a tricky word. • Ask the children to tell you the 'tricky bit'. Ask them to spell the word. • Write the word on the board and ask the children to check their spelling of it carefully. Ask them to fix any errors.	• Choose either a GPC or a word from the book, depending on the needs of the children. • Observe the children as they write to check for misspellings. • Model writing the GPC/word. Draw attention to the correct spelling of any part that the children spelled incorrectly. • For words: Model again how to count the sounds and how to spell each grapheme. • If a child still spells the GPC/word incorrectly, make a note and ensure they have additional practice during the day.

All phases: Reading the 7+ books – comprehension

You will need: Grapheme cards for the GPCs covered in the book.

In advance of the lesson: Download the focus words, tricky words, vocabulary and comprehension guidance from collins.co.uk/BigCatLittleWandleL&SRevised.

Pre-read

What to do	Notes
Quick review • Carry out a quick review of any GPCs, words or tricky words that the children need practice with, as identified in the decoding and prosody sessions. • Tell the children you want them to read the words quickly.	• The children should read these words quickly and commit them to their long-term memory (orthographic store). • If children cannot read a tricky word, identify the 'tricky bit' by pointing to the tricky grapheme and saying its sound. • Look out for any children who are not able to say the words with automaticity, and provide additional support outside of the lesson.

Practise and apply

What to do	Notes
Read the book • The reading should be even quicker this time. • Ask the children to read independently. • Ask them to read the words without sounding out each word aloud, but remind them they can sound out and blend words if they need to. • If you are working with more than one child, tap in to listen to each child read, and check that they are reading every word. **Comprehension** • Use the teaching notes in the back of the book for further support or download the additional guidance and example questions from the Collins website. • Ask each question. Ask the children to read independently to find the answer. • Give the children thinking time and then choose a child to answer. • If the answer is correct, ask all the children to point to the answer. If the answer is incorrect, acknowledge the child's effort and then take responses from other children in the group. • Explain how you know the answer is correct. **Say:** *I know this because...* Point to where the answer is in the text. • Continue to ask the other questions.	• In the early stages, you may want to direct the children to a particular page or section of the book to look for the answer. • Once the children have attempted the answer, model and scaffold how the answer was found. • In these comprehension activities, encourage the children to integrate their knowledge of pictures and words to answer the questions. • Always ensure the children use decoding strategies to read words, rather than guessing. • Ask the children to point to words to answer retrieval questions. • Encourage the children to answer in sentences and be precise in their answers, e.g. *Which word tells you that?*
Home reading • Remind the children they are taking the book home to practise reading it and that they need to bring it back the next day. • Tell them you want them to practise reading fluently and with prosody.	• Remember, the purpose of all home reading at this stage is to develop confident, fluent, independent reading and provide positive encouragement. • If needed, remind the children what to do if they are not able to read a word: sound out the graphemes and blend. But, if possible, they should try to blend in their heads.

Phase 2 grapheme chart

Grapheme card	Picture card	Pronunciation phrase
s	s	Show your teeth and let the **s** hiss out **sssss sssss**
a	a	Open your mouth wide and make the **a** sound at the back of your mouth **a a a**
t	t	Open your lips; put the tip of your tongue behind your teeth and press **t t t**
p	p	Bring your lips together, push them open and say **p p p**
i	i	Pull your lips back and make the **i** sound at the back of your mouth **i i i**
n	n	Open your lips a bit; put your tongue behind your teeth and make the **nnnnn** sound **nnnnn**
m	m	Put your lips together and make the **mmmmm** sound **mmmmm**
d	d	Put your tongue to the top and front of your mouth and make a quick **d** sound **d d d**
g	g	Give me a big smile that shows your teeth; press the middle of your tongue to the top and back of your mouth; push your tongue down and forward to make the **g** sound **g g g**
o	o	Make your mouth into a round shape and say **o o o**

Grapheme card	Picture card	Pronunciation phrase
c	(cat)	Open your mouth into a little smile; make your tongue flat and move it up towards the top of your mouth to say **c c c**
k	(kite)	Open your mouth into a little smile; make your tongue flat and move it up towards the top of your mouth to say **k k k**
ck	(sock)	Open your mouth into a little smile; make your tongue flat and move it up towards the top of your mouth to say **c c c**
e	(elephant)	Open your mouth wide and say **e e e**
u	(umbrella)	Open your mouth wide and say **u u u**
r	(rainbow)	Show me your teeth to make a **rrrr** sound **rrrrr**
h	(helicopter)	Open your mouth and breathe out sharply **h h h**
b	(bear)	Put your lips together and say **b** as you open them **b b b**
f	(flamingo)	Open your lips a little; put your teeth on your bottom lip and push the air out to make the sound **ffffff ffffff**
l	(lollipop)	Open your mouth a little; put your tongue up to the top of your mouth, behind your teeth, and press **llll llll llll**
j	(jellyfish)	Pucker your lips and show your teeth; use your tongue as you say **j j j**

Grapheme card	Picture card	Pronunciation phrase
v	(volcano)	Put your teeth against your bottom lip and make a buzzing sound **vvvv vvvv**
w	(waves)	Pucker your lips and keep them small as you say **w w w**
x	(x box)	Mouth open, then push the **cs/x** sound through as you close your mouth **cs cs cs** (**x x x**)
y	(yo-yo)	Smile, tongue to the top of your mouth; say **y** without opening your mouth **y y y**
z	(zebra)	Show me your teeth and buzz the **z** sound **zzzzzz zzzzzz**
qu	(queen)	Pucker your mouth, then open it as you say **qu qu qu**
ch	(cherries)	Pucker your lips and show your teeth; use your tongue as you say **ch ch ch**
sh	(shell)	Show me your teeth and push the air out **shshshshsh**
th	(thumb)	Voiced: Tongue on your teeth, teeth almost closed to make a 'buzzing' **th th th** Unvoiced: Tongue on your teeth, push the air out **th th th**
ng	(ring)	Open your mouth a bit and then use your tongue at the back of your mouth to say **ng ng ng**
nk	(panda)	Open your mouth a bit and then use your tongue at the back of your mouth to say **nk nk nk**

List of Phase 4 words

Adjacent consonant and short vowel sounds

CVCC
must wind best hand
lunch gift nest help

CCVC
bring crack frog drink
drum truck swim spend

CCVCC
twist grand stamp crisp

CCCVC
split splash spring strong

CCCVCC
strand scrunch sprint strict

Adjacent consonant and long vowel sounds

CVCC
joint toast paint burnt
boost

CCVC
brown sport bright green
broom crown train greed

CCV
clear stair tree star three

CCVCC
spoilt

CCCVC
sprain street screens

Phase 5 linked graphemes in order

Week 1

Phase 3 GPC	Phase 5 GPC
ai	ay play
ow	ou cloud
oi	oy toy
ee	ea each
ur er	ir bird
oo yoo	ue blue rescue

Week 2

Phase 3 GPC	Phase 5 GPC	
oo yoo	ue blue rescue	u unicorn
igh	ie pie	i tiger
oa	o go	
ai	ay play	a paper
ee	ea each	e he

Week 3

Phase 3 GPC	Phase 5 GPC			
oa	o go	o-e home		
ai	ay play	a paper	a-e shake	
ee	ea each	e he	e-e these	
igh	ie pie	i tiger	i-e time	
oo yoo	ue blue rescue	u unicorn	u-e rude cute	ew chew new

Week 4

Phase 2/3 GPC	Phase 5 GPC				
or	aw claw				
ee	ea each	e he	e-e these	ie shield	y funny
e	ea head				
w	wh wheel				
igh	ie pie	i tiger	i-e time	y fly	

Week 5

Phase 2/3 GPC	Phase 5 GPC				
oa	o go	o-e home	oe toe	ou shoulder	ow snow
j	g giant				
f	ph phone				
s	c ice				

Week 6

Phase 2 GPC	Phase 5 GPC		
l	le apple	al metal	
v	ve give		
u	o-e some	o mother	ou young

Week 7

Phase 2/3 GPC	Phase 5 GPC					
z	se cheese					
s	c ice	se mouse	ce fence			
ee	ea each	e he	e-e these	ie shield	y funny	ey donkey
oo yoo	ue blue rescue	u unicorn	u-e rude cute	ew chew new	ui fruit	ou soup

Week 8

Phase 3 GPC	Phase 5 GPC		
ur er	ir bird	or word	
oo	u awful	oul could	
air	are share	ear bear	ere there

Week 9

Phase 3 GPC	Phase 5 GPC					
or	aw claw	au author	aur dinosaur	oor floor	al walk	a water
ch	tch match	ture adventure				

Week 10

Phase 2/3 GPC	Phase 5 GPC	
ar	al half	a father
o	a want	
ur	ear learn	
r	wr wrist	
z	se cheese	ze freeze

Week 11

Phase 2/3 GPC	Phase 5 GPC				
s	c ice	se mouse	ce fence	st whistle	sc science
c	ch school				
sh	ch chef				

Week 12

Phase 2/3 GPC	Phase 5 GPC						
ai	ay play	a paper	a-e shake	eigh eight	aigh straight	ey grey	ea break
n	kn knee	gn gnaw					
m	mb thumb						

Week 13

Phase 2/3 GPC	Phase 5 GPC						
ear	ere here	eer deer					
zh	su treasure	si vision					
j	g giant	dge bridge	ge large				
i	y crystal						

Week 14

Phase 2/3 GPC	Phase 5 GPC						
sh	ch chef	ti potion	ssi mission	si mansion	ci delicious		
or	aw claw	au author	aur dinosaur	al walk	oor floor	a water	augh daughter our your oar board ore more

Graphemes with more than one sound

List of graphemes that have more than one phoneme for: **Reading words with GPCs that have more than one sound, e.g. 'ow' /ow/ /oa/** (page 47). Images to represent the example Phase 5 sounds are available on the website.

Grapheme	Phase 2 and 3 mnemonic/catchphrase	Phase 5 example words/images			
a	astronaut	/ai/ paper	/or/ water	/o/ wash	/ar/ father
e	elephant	/ee/ fever			
i	iguana	/igh/ spider			
o	octopus	/oa/ post	/u/ son		
u	umbrella	/yoo/ unicorn	/oo/ pudding		
ow	owl /ow/ wow owl	/oa/ snow			
ou	n/a	/ow/ cloud	/oa/ shoulder	/u/ touch	/oo/ soup
ey	n/a	/ee/ donkey	/ai/ grey		
ea	n/a	/ee/ beach	/e/ head	/ai/ break	
ie	n/a	/igh/ pie	/ee/ shield		
o-e	n/a	/oa/ nose	/u/ love		
al	n/a	/l/ petal	/or/ chalk	/ar/ half	
y	yo-yo	/ee/ baby	/igh/ fly	/i/ crystal	
g	goat	/j/ gem			
c	cat	/s/ ice			
or	horn /or/ born with a horn	/ur/ world			
ear	hear /ear/ get near to hear	/air/ bear	/ur/ search		
ere	n/a	/air/ there	/ear/ sphere		
ch	cherry /ch/ chew the cherries children	/c/ school	/sh/ chef		
se	n/a	/s/ mouse	/z/ cheese		
si	n/a	/zh/ television	/sh/ mansion		

Precision teaching grids